MAURITIUS TRAVEL GUIDE 2025

Mauritius for Every Traveler: A tailored companion for Honeymooners, Families, Solo Adventurers, and Budget Explorers Without Overspending

Jenny M. Dobson

Mauritius Travel Guide 2025

WELCOME TO MAURITIUS

Copyright © 2025 by Jenny M. Dobson

All rights reserved.

Except for brief quotations that are incorporated into reviews and certain other noncommercial uses that are permitted by copyright law, no portion of this book may be reproduced, distributed, or transmitted in any form or by any means, including photocopying, recording, or other electronic or mechanical methods, without the prior written permission of the author. This includes, but is not limited to, this book.

Disclaimer

The information provided in *Mauritius Travel Guide 2025* is intended to serve as a helpful resource for travelers seeking to explore Mauritius. While every effort has been made to ensure the accuracy, reliability, and completeness of the information contained within this book, travel-related details such as prices, opening hours, visa requirements, transportation schedules, and local regulations are subject to change at any time. Readers are encouraged to verify critical information with official sources, such as government agencies, tourism boards, transportation providers, and local businesses, before making any travel arrangements.

The author and publisher have made every reasonable attempt to present current and accurate details at the time of writing. However, due to the dynamic nature of travel, unforeseen circumstances—such as changes in government policies, weather conditions, business closures, or economic fluctuations—may affect the availability of certain services or experiences described in this book. Neither the author nor the publisher can be held responsible for any inaccuracies, omissions, or unexpected changes that may arise after publication.

This guide is based on research, local insights, and personal recommendations, but it is not an exhaustive or definitive source on Mauritius. The information, suggestions, and recommendations are provided for general informational purposes only and should not be interpreted as professional advice. Travelers are encouraged to exercise their own judgment and discretion when making decisions regarding their itinerary, safety, and overall experience.

Additionally, the author and publisher do not assume any responsibility or liability for any loss, inconvenience, injury, damage, or expense that may result from using this book or relying on the information provided. Travelers are advised to take appropriate precautions, including securing necessary travel insurance, adhering to local laws and customs, and being aware of potential risks associated with activities such as hiking, water sports, or wildlife encounters.

This book may contain references to third-party businesses, services, and products. Any mention of hotels, restaurants, tour operators, or other establishments does not constitute an endorsement or guarantee of quality.

The experiences of individual travelers may vary, and readers are encouraged to conduct their own research or read recent reviews before making bookings or purchases.

By using this guide, readers acknowledge and accept that travel inherently involves risks, and they assume full responsibility for their own choices and experiences. The author and publisher disclaim any liability for reliance on the information provided in this book.

Thank you for your understanding, and may your journey to Mauritius be filled with incredible discoveries and unforgettable moments.

TABLE OF CONTENT

HOW TO USE THIS GUIDE...12
CHAPTER ONE..17
MAURITIUS AT A GLANCE..17
CHAPTER TWO... 27
PLANNING YOUR TRIP TO MAURITIUS................................... 27
CHAPTER THREE... 37
EXPERIENCES FOR EVERY KIND OF TRAVELER....................37
ACCOMMODATIONS IN MAURITIUS...95
CHAPTER FOUR... 103
ACCOMMODATIONS IN MAURITIUS...103

CHAPTER FIVE.. 112
TRANSPORTATION AND GETTING AROUND........................112
CHAPTER SIX..122
TOP ATTRACTIONS AND THINGS TO DO............................. 122
CHAPTER SEVEN... 156
CULINARY DELIGHTS OF MAURITIUS.....................................156
CHAPTER EIGHT.. 172
SHOPPING IN MAURITIUS..172
CHAPTER NINE.. 181
OUTDOOR ADVENTURES AND ACTIVITIES.........................181

CHAPTER TEN	190
OUTDOOR ADVENTURES IN MAURITIUS:	190
CHAPTER ELEVEN	198
MAURITIUS' CULTURAL AND FESTIVE SCENE	198
CHAPTER ELEVEN	207
HEALTH, SAFETY, AND PRACTICAL INFORMATION	207
CHAPTER TWELVE	216
DAY TRIPS AND EXCURSIONS	216
CHAPTER THIRTEEN	225
SAMPLE ITINERARIES	225
CHAPTER FOURTEEN	234
SUSTAINABILITY AND RESPONSIBLE TOURISM IN MAURITIUS	234
CHAPTER FIFTEEN	244
USEFUL CONTACTS AND RESOURCES FOR TRAVELERS IN MAURITIUS	244
CHAPTER SIXTEEN	254
RECOMMENDED TOUR OPERATORS AND GUIDES, ONLINE RESOURCES, AND APPS FOR TRAVELERS	254

Dear Traveler,

Welcome to *Mauritius Travel Guide 2025*! I'm truly honored that you've chosen this book as your companion for exploring one of the most breathtaking destinations on Earth. Your trust means the world to me, and I want to start by expressing my deepest gratitude for allowing me to be part of your travel journey.

Traveling is more than just visiting new places—it's about immersing yourself in cultures, savoring new flavors, meeting incredible people, and creating unforgettable memories. And Mauritius? Well, this island is pure magic.

Whether you're dreaming of lounging on pristine beaches, diving into its rich history, indulging in delicious Creole cuisine, or seeking thrilling adventures, I promise you—this book will guide you every step of the way.

I have poured my heart into crafting this guide with the most up-to-date, insightful, and practical information, making sure it's more than just a book—it's your personal travel companion. Inside, you'll find hidden gems, local secrets, and must-know tips that will help you experience Mauritius in the most authentic and fulfilling way possible. I want you to feel like an explorer, not just a visitor.

No matter if this is your first time in Mauritius or your tenth, my goal is to ensure this guide enhances your journey, simplifies your planning, and helps you fall in love with the island in a way you never expected. This book was written with passion, dedication, and a deep appreciation for the beauty of travel—and I sincerely hope it becomes one of the best travel guides you've ever used.

Thank you for allowing me to be part of your adventure. I can't wait for you to experience the wonders of Mauritius, and I truly hope this guide helps you make the most of every moment.

Wishing you safe travels, incredible discoveries, and a journey filled with joy.

Happy exploring!

With gratitude,

Jenny M. Dobson

HOW TO USE THIS GUIDE

Welcome to *Mauritius Travel Guide 2025!* Whether you're a first-time visitor or a seasoned traveler returning to this breathtaking island, this guide is designed to provide you with **comprehensive, up-to-date**, and **easy-to-navigate** information.

This book is more than just a collection of travel tips—it's your **trusted companion** to exploring Mauritius in 2025. You'll find insider insights, essential travel details, and practical recommendations tailored to different types of travelers.

Overview of Guide Features

To make your journey seamless and stress-free, this guide is packed with features that ensure you get the most out of your trip. Here's what to expect:

■ **Detailed Destination Insights** – Explore Mauritius beyond the typical tourist spots with in-depth coverage of **hidden gems, cultural sites, beaches, hiking trails, and culinary delights.**

■ **Updated Travel Information for 2025** – Get the latest details on **entry requirements, visa policies, currency** exchange, safety tips, and health regulations** to help you plan confidently.

■ **Customized Itineraries** – Whether you have **three days or two weeks**, you'll find **flexible, curated itineraries** based on different travel styles—family vacations, adventure seekers, honeymooners, and solo explorers.

■ **Local Recommendations** – From the **best street food stalls in Port Louis** to **luxury resorts in Grand Baie**, discover recommendations curated with insights from **locals and experienced travelers.**

■ **Responsible & Sustainable Travel Advice** – Learn how to **respect local customs**, support eco-friendly tourism, and experience Mauritius **responsibly and ethically** in 2025.

Navigating Chapters for Different Types of Travelers

This book is structured to cater to all kinds of travelers, ensuring **you can quickly find what matters most to you**. Here's how you can navigate the guide efficiently:

■ **If you're visiting Mauritius for the first time:** Start with the *Essential Travel Information* and *Top Attractions* sections to get a broad understanding of what the island offers.

■ **If you're a beach lover:** Head straight to the *Best Beaches & Coastal Adventures* chapter to find the most picturesque and secluded spots.

■ **If you love adventure and nature:** Explore the *Outdoor Activities & Eco-Tourism* section for hiking trails, diving spots, and wildlife encounters.

■ **If you're a foodie:** Check out the *Mauritian Cuisine & Dining Guide* for the best places to try authentic Creole, Indian, Chinese, and French-influenced dishes.

■ **If you want a luxurious escape:** The *Luxury Travel & Wellness Retreats* chapter will introduce you to **high-end** resorts, private island experiences, and world-class spa treatments.

▪ **If you're on a budget:** The *Budget Travel Tips* section covers affordable stays, low-cost activities, and how to enjoy Mauritius without breaking the bank.

▪ **If you're a history and culture enthusiast:** The *History, Culture & Local Traditions* chapter dives into the island's **rich past, colonial influences, and vibrant festivals.**

Tips for Using Maps, Recommendations, and Contact Information

To enhance your travel experience, this guide includes **practical resources** to help you navigate Mauritius with ease:

Consider downloading **offline maps** before arrival to avoid roaming charges.

▪ **Recommendations** – Each section includes carefully selected **recommendations for hotels, restaurants, and activities,** along with approximate costs and best times to visit.

📞 **Important Contact Information** – Find essential contacts, including **embassies, emergency services, hospitals, and transport hotlines**, ensuring you're prepared for any situation.

💡 **QR Codes & Online Resources** – Scan QR codes (where available) for **updated websites, booking links, and real-time travel alerts**.

Final Thoughts

This guide is structured to be **your go-to resource** for an unforgettable trip to Mauritius in 2025. Whether you're looking for adventure, relaxation, or cultural exploration, this book has been designed to help you **maximize your experience** and create lasting memories.

Now, let's dive into the heart of Mauritius and start planning your **dream getaway!** 🚀 🌴

CHAPTER ONE
MAURITIUS AT A GLANCE

A Brief Introduction to Mauritius: History, Geography, and Culture

Welcome to Paradise

Mauritius, a breathtaking island nation in the **Indian Ocean**, is a dream destination known for its **pristine beaches, turquoise lagoons, lush mountains, and diverse cultural heritage**. Whether you're looking for adventure, relaxation, or a deep dive into history and local traditions, Mauritius offers an **unforgettable experience** for every traveler.

A Glimpse into the Past

Though Mauritius is often associated with idyllic scenery, its history is just as fascinating. The island was **uninhabited** until the early 16th century when **Portuguese explorers** first arrived. However, it was the **Dutch (1598-1710)** who named the island after Prince Maurice of Nassau. They introduced sugarcane but left after struggling with harsh conditions.

The **French (1715-1810)** took control next, renaming it *Île de France* and developing the sugarcane industry, which remains an essential part of the economy today.

The British **seized Mauritius in 1810** and ruled until **independence in 1968.** Under British governance, slavery was abolished in **1835**, leading to the arrival of indentured laborers from **India**, who played a significant role in shaping the island's **multicultural identity.**

Today, Mauritius is a **thriving democracy**, known for its **political stability, economic progress, and rich cultural diversity.** The island is home to **Hindus, Creoles, Muslims, Chinese, and Europeans**, creating a **harmonious blend of traditions, languages, and festivals** that make Mauritius truly special.

Geography: More Than Just Beaches

Mauritius is a **volcanic island**, covering **2,040 square kilometers (788 square miles).** It sits about **2,000 kilometers (1,242 miles) off the southeast coast of Africa**, near **Madagascar, Réunion, and Rodrigues.**

Beyond the postcard-perfect beaches, Mauritius boasts:

- **Mountainous interiors** – including the **Black River Gorges National Park**, home to waterfalls, rainforests, and exotic wildlife.

Mauritius Travel Guide 2025

- **Coral reefs** – surrounding the island, providing excellent snorkeling and diving opportunities.

- **Small offshore islands** – such as **Île aux Cerfs**, **Île aux Aigrettes**, and **Gabriel Island**, perfect for day trips.

Culture: A Fusion of Influences

Mauritius is a **melting pot of cultures**, influenced by **Indian, African, French, and Chinese traditions**. This unique blend is reflected in **music, dance, cuisine, and religious festivals**.

- **Music & Dance**: The **Sega** is Mauritius' most famous dance and music style, originating from enslaved Africans. With its rhythmic beats and colorful performances, Sega tells stories of struggle, joy, and resilience.

- **Festivals**: The island celebrates **Hindu festivals like Diwali and Maha Shivaratri, Chinese New Year, Muslim Eid celebrations**, and **Christian Christmas and Easter**, all with **equal enthusiasm**.

- **Cuisine**: Mauritian food is a delightful mix of **Indian curries, Creole seafood, Chinese noodles, and French pastries**. Don't miss **dholl puri, boulettes (dumplings), gateau piment (chili cakes), and fresh seafood platters**.

Fast Facts: Currency, Language, Population, and Climate

Essential Travel Information

Here are some quick facts to help you navigate Mauritius:

🪙 **Currency**: The **Mauritian Rupee (MUR)** − 1 USD ≈ **45 MUR** *(exchange rates fluctuate, so check before traveling).*

- **Languages**: The official language is **English**, but **French and Mauritian Creole** are widely spoken. Many locals also speak **Bhojpuri, Hindi, Tamil, and Mandarin**.

- **Population**: Approximately **1.3 million people**, making it one of the most densely populated islands in the world.

- **Time Zone**: Mauritius Standard Time (MUT), UTC+4 (no daylight-saving time).

- **Country Code**: +230 (use this for making local calls).

- **Electricity**: 230V, 50Hz – plug types **C and G** (bring an adapter if needed).

- **Driving**: **Left-hand drive** (British system). Renting a car is easy, but be prepared for **narrow roads and occasional traffic in urban areas**.

Climate: When to Visit?

Mauritius has a **tropical climate**, meaning **warm temperatures year-round** with distinct seasons:

- ☀ **Summer (November–April)**: Hot and humid, perfect for beachgoers and water sports enthusiasts. Expect temperatures between **25-33°C (77-91°F)**.

- 🌴 **Cyclone Season (January–March):** While rare, tropical cyclones can occur, bringing heavy rains and strong winds.

- 🍃 **Winter (May–October):** Cooler and drier, with pleasant temperatures ranging from **17-26°C (63-79°F)**. Ideal for **hiking, sightseeing, and cultural exploration**.

Best Time to Visit:

- For **beaches & snorkeling:** October to April
- For **hiking & sightseeing:** May to October
- For **whale watching:** July to September

Key Highlights: What Makes Mauritius Unique?

Why choose Mauritius over other tropical destinations? Here are some standout reasons:

🌴 **World-Class Beaches** – From the lively shores of **Grand Baie** to the untouched beauty of **Le Morne**, the island offers **powdery white sands and crystal-clear waters**.

🐚 **Rich Marine Life & Coral Reefs** – Snorkel or dive at **Blue Bay Marine Park, Île aux Cerfs, and Belle Mare** to see colorful fish, dolphins, and even whales.

🏝️ **Private Islands & Hidden Paradises** – Explore remote gems like **Île aux Aigrettes**, a conservation island home to rare birds and giant tortoises.

🍲 **Gastronomic Delights** – A paradise for food lovers, blending Indian spices, French techniques, and Creole traditions.

🏞️ **Diverse Landscapes** – Whether it's **hiking in Black River Gorges**, climbing **Le Morne Brabant**, or exploring **Chamarel's Seven-Colored Earth**, Mauritius is more than just beaches.

🏋♂ **Adventure Awaits** – From kitesurfing in **Le Morne** to deep-sea fishing and zip-lining in **Casela Nature Park**, Mauritius is an adventure lover's dream.

🍂 **Cultural Harmony** – Witness **Hindu temples, colonial-era churches, mosques, and Chinese pagodas** coexisting peacefully.

Must-See Attractions: Top Landmarks, Beaches, and Nature Spots

✔ **Le Morne Brabant** – A UNESCO World Heritage site with cultural significance and stunning views.

✔ **Black River Gorges National Park** – The best spot for hiking, wildlife spotting, and nature photography.

✔ **Île aux Cerfs** – The ultimate tropical island escape with water sports and pristine beaches.

✔ **Chamarel Seven-Colored Earth** – A surreal natural phenomenon with rainbow-colored sand dunes.

✔ **Pamplemousses Botanical Garden** – Home to giant water lilies, exotic plants, and century-old trees.

✔ **Port Louis** – The lively capital, featuring **Central Market, Caudan Waterfront, and the Blue Penny Museum.**

✔ **Grand Baie** – Mauritius' most popular tourist hub with vibrant nightlife, restaurants, and beaches.

✔ **Trou aux Biches & Belle Mare** – Two of the island's best beaches for **swimming, sunbathing, and relaxation.**

Final Thoughts

Mauritius is more than just a beach destination—it's a **cultural melting pot, an adventure hub, and a nature lover's paradise.** Whether you're here for relaxation, discovery, or a mix of both, this island promises an **unforgettable experience in 2025.**

Ready to explore Mauritius further? Let's dive into the next chapter! ●✈

CHAPTER TWO
PLANNING YOUR TRIP TO MAURITIUS

Planning a trip to Mauritius is an exciting journey in itself. Whether you're traveling for **a romantic getaway, a family vacation, or an adventure-filled escape**, knowing the best time to visit, visa requirements, budget considerations, packing essentials, and eco-friendly travel practices can **make your trip seamless and stress-free**.

When to Visit: Best Seasons and Weather Insights

Mauritius enjoys a **tropical climate**, meaning **warm temperatures year-round**, but different seasons can offer unique experiences. Choosing the right time to visit depends on your **interests, activities, and weather preferences**.

Mauritius' Seasons at a Glance

Summer (November–April) ✺

> Hot and humid, perfect for **beach lovers, snorkeling, and diving**.
>
> Average temperature: **25-33°C (77-91°F)**.
>
> **Best for:** Water activities, deep-sea fishing, island hopping, and exploring marine life.

Keep in mind: **Cyclone season peaks from January to March,** bringing occasional storms.

Winter (May–October) ❄

Cooler and drier, ideal for **hiking, sightseeing, and cultural exploration.**

Average temperature: **17–26°C (63–79°F)**.

Best for: Exploring national parks, trekking, and experiencing local festivals.

Keep in mind: The sea can be a bit cooler, but still comfortable for swimming.

Best Time to Visit Based on Your Interests

- **For beach lovers:** October to April (warm waters and calm seas).

- **For hikers and nature enthusiasts:** May to October (cooler temperatures and clear trails).

- **For diving and snorkeling:** December to March (best underwater visibility).

- **For whale watching:** July to September (sperm and humpback whales migrate through Mauritian waters).

- **For cultural experiences**: Visit during major festivals like **Diwali (October/November), Chinese New Year (January/February)**, or Independence Day (March 12th).

No matter when you visit, Mauritius is **a paradise in every season**, but planning according to the activities you love will make your trip even more special.

Visa and Entry Requirements: Essential Paperwork and Guidelines

Do You Need a Visa?

Mauritius is **visa-free or offers visa-on-arrival for travelers from over 100 countries**. However, regulations change, so it's always best to **check with your nearest Mauritian embassy or consulate** before traveling.

Visa-Free & Visa-on-Arrival Countries

- **No Visa Required**: Citizens from the **EU, UK, USA, Canada, Australia, New Zealand, and most African & Asian countries** can stay for **up to 90 days** visa-free.

- **Visa on Arrival**: Some travelers, including those from **Russia and China**, can obtain a **visa upon arrival** for stays of up to **60 days**.

- **E-Visa Option**: Some nationalities may need to apply online before traveling.

Entry Requirements for All Travelers

Regardless of visa status, visitors must have:

✔ A **passport valid for at least six months** beyond their stay.

✔ A **return ticket** or proof of onward travel.

✔ Proof of accommodation (hotel booking or invitation letter from a host).

✔ Sufficient funds to cover expenses during the stay.

Health & COVID-19 Regulations: While most **COVID-19 travel restrictions have been lifted**, it's always best to check for **updated health guidelines** before your departure. Some vaccinations, such as **yellow fever**, may be required if you're coming from an affected country.

Budgeting Your Trip: Cost Estimates for All Budgets

Mauritius caters to **all types of travelers**, from budget backpackers to luxury seekers. Below is a rough estimate of what you can expect to spend per day based on your travel style.

Daily Budget Estimates

Travel Style	Budget Traveler 💰	Mid-Range 💼	Luxury Traveler 💎
Accommodation	$20 - $50 (guesthouses, hostels)	$80 - $150 (3-4 star hotels)	$250+ (5-star resorts, private villas)
Food & Drinks	$5 - $15 (local street food, small cafes)	$20 - $50 (casual restaurants)	$80+ (fine dining, hotel buffets)
Transport	$2 - $10 (buses, shared taxis)	$30 - $50 (car rental, private taxi)	$100+ (chauffeur, private transfers)

| Activities | $10 - $30 (hiking, free attractions) | $50 - $100 (snorkeling, cultural tours) | $200+ (private boat tours, helicopter rides) |

Tips for Budget Travelers:

🕯 Use **public transport** instead of taxis.

🕯 Eat at **local food stalls and markets** (try dholl puri and mine bouille).

🕯 Stay in **guesthouses or Airbnb** instead of resorts.

🕯 Enjoy **free attractions** like **public beaches, hiking trails, and temples**.

Tips for Mid-Range Travelers:

🕯 Book hotels **with included breakfast** to save on food costs.

🕯 Rent a **car for flexible and affordable island exploration**.

🕯 Look for **combo deals on excursions and activities**.

Tips for Luxury Travelers:

- Consider **all-inclusive resorts** for hassle-free luxury.
- Book a **private island-hopping tour** for an exclusive experience.
- Indulge in **spa treatments, fine dining, and yacht cruises**.

Regardless of your budget, **Mauritius has something for everyone!**

Packing Checklist: What to Bring for a Comfortable Vacation

Packing smart can make all the difference in **ensuring a stress-free and enjoyable stay.**

Essential Items for All Travelers

- **Travel Documents** – Passport, visa (if needed), travel insurance, accommodation confirmations.
- **Lightweight Clothing** – Breathable fabrics for warm days, and a light jacket for cooler nights.
- **Footwear** – Sandals for the beach, comfortable walking shoes for sightseeing, and water shoes for reefs.
- **Sun Protection** – Sunscreen, sunglasses, hat, and after-sun lotion.

🦟 **Insect Repellent** – Mosquitoes can be a nuisance, especially in humid areas.

📷 **Camera / GoPro** – Capture Mauritius' beauty both on land and underwater.

💧 **Reusable Water Bottle** – Stay hydrated while reducing plastic waste.

🩱 **Swimwear & Snorkeling Gear** – Many beaches and lagoons are great for snorkeling right off the shore.

🔌 **Universal Adapter** – Mauritius uses **Type C and G plugs (230V)**.

Optional But Useful Items

🎒 **Dry Bag** – Great for keeping electronics safe during water activities.

🚗 **International Driver's License** – If you plan to rent a car.

🛍️ **Extra Bag** – For souvenirs like **local rum, handcrafted jewelry, and spices**.

Sustainable Travel Tips: Eco-Friendly Practices for Visitors

Mauritius is **one of the world's most beautiful islands**, but it faces environmental challenges such as **coral reef** degradation, plastic pollution, and deforestation. Responsible tourism can **help preserve its beauty** for future generations.

How to Travel Sustainably in Mauritius

🌿 **Avoid Single-Use Plastics** – Carry a **reusable water bottle and shopping bag.**

🐢 **Respect Marine Life** – Avoid stepping on corals and choose **reef-safe sunscreen.**

🗑 **Dispose of Waste Properly** – Use **recycling bins** and support eco-friendly businesses.

🚲 **Use Eco-Friendly Transport** – Consider **cycling, walking, or public buses** to reduce your carbon footprint.

🍽 **Eat & Shop Local** – Support small businesses, local markets, and eco-conscious accommodations.

🏕 **Stay in Green Hotels** – Many lodges and resorts focus on **sustainable tourism** initiatives.

By making small eco-friendly choices, you can contribute to **preserving Mauritius' natural beauty** while still having an incredible time.

Final Thoughts

Proper planning can make your **Mauritian adventure smooth and unforgettable.** Whether you're looking for a **budget-friendly escape or a luxurious retreat,** this guide ensures you're **fully prepared** for the journey ahead.

Next up, let's explore **how to get around Mauritius and uncover the best travel routes!** 🚙✈

CHAPTER THREE
EXPERIENCES FOR EVERY KIND OF TRAVELER

Mauritius is a **versatile paradise**, offering something for everyone—whether you crave **luxury, adventure, or a mix of both**. From **world-class resorts and private villas** to **thrilling water sports and scenic hikes**, this chapter highlights **tailor-made experiences** that cater to different travel styles.

For Luxury Travelers: Indulgence in Paradise

If you're looking for **exquisite comfort, world-class hospitality, and exclusive experiences**, Mauritius won't disappoint. With **high-end beachfront resorts, private villas, luxury spas, and gourmet dining**, the island offers an **unparalleled escape for those who appreciate the finer things in life**.

High-End Resorts: Top Picks with Contact Information

Mauritius boasts some of the **world's most luxurious resorts**, offering **unrivaled service, private beaches, and breathtaking ocean views**. Here are some of the best:

1. One&Only Le Saint Géran (Belle Mare) ★★★★★

🏝 Why Stay Here?

- Iconic **5-star beachfront resort** with **private pools and butler service**.
- Exclusive **overwater dining experiences** and a **world-class golf course**.
- Signature **spa treatments** and water sports activities.

📍 **Location:** Belle Mare, East Coast
📞 **Phone:** +230 401 1688
🌐 **Website:** www.oneandonlyresorts.com

2. The St. Regis Mauritius Resort (Le Morne) ★★★★★

♣ **Why Stay Here?**

- Elegant colonial-style architecture with **personalized butler service**.
- Pristine beachfront location with **stunning views of Le Morne Brabant Mountain**.
- Exclusive spa treatments and **Michelin-starred dining**.

📍 **Location:** Le Morne Peninsula, Southwest Mauritius
📞 **Phone:** +230 403 9000
🌐 **Website:** www.marriott.com

3. Four Seasons Resort Mauritius at Anahita (Beau Champ)
★★★★★

♣ **Why Stay Here?**

- Luxurious **private villas with infinity pools**.
- Access to **Ile aux Cerfs Golf Club**, one of the **best golf courses in the world**.
- World-class **spa, fitness center, and wellness programs**.

📍 **Location:** Beau Champ, East Coast
📞 **Phone:** +230 402 3100
🌐 **Website:** www.fourseasons.com

4. Royal Palm Beachcomber Luxury (Grand Baie)

★★★★★

🏖 Why Stay Here?

- **Exclusive boutique luxury experience** with only 69 suites.
- Fine dining at **La Goélette**, a **Michelin-starred restaurant**.
- Unparalleled **personalized service** in an intimate setting.

📍 **Location:** Grand Baie, North Coast
📞 **Phone:** +230 209 8300
🌐 **Website:** www.beachcomber-hotels.com

Private Villas and Exclusive Experiences

For those who prefer **complete privacy**, renting a **private villa** is the ultimate indulgence. These luxurious hideaways offer **personal chefs, infinity pools, and stunning ocean views**, ensuring a **tailor-made holiday experience**.

Top Private Villas in Mauritius

🏝 **Villa One by One&Only** (Belle Mare)

- **Ultra-luxurious villa** with a **private infinity pool and dedicated staff**.
- Perfect for **honeymooners and VIP guests**.

🏝 **Oasis Villas by Evaco** (Grand Baie)

- **Elegant Balinese-style villas** with **private gardens and pools**.
- **Butler service and in-villa spa treatments** available.

🏝 **Heritage The Villas** (Bel Ombre)

- **Luxury beachfront residences** with access to **a golf course and private beaches**.
- Ideal for families and long-term stays.

Unique Luxury Experiences in Mauritius

✦ **Private Catamaran Cruises** – Enjoy a **VIP sailing experience**, complete with **champagne, gourmet meals, and snorkeling stops**.

✦ **Helicopter Island Tours** – Marvel at the **aerial view of Mauritius**, including the **famous underwater waterfall illusion**.

✦ **Sunset Horseback Riding on the Beach** – Ride along **Le Morne's** pristine shores at sunset for a **romantic experience**.

Spa Retreats and Fine Dining Recommendations

Mauritius is home to some of the **best wellness retreats** in the Indian Ocean. Whether you want a **detox retreat**, **Ayurvedic treatments, or holistic healing sessions**, you'll find **world-class spas** that cater to your needs.

Best Luxury Spas in Mauritius

🌿 **The Oberoi Spa (Turtle Bay)** – Offers **traditional Mauritian therapies and aromatherapy massages** in a secluded, nature-filled setting.

🌿 **Shanti Maurice Spa (Chemin Grenier)** – Specializes in **Ayurvedic and wellness retreats**, with **oceanfront meditation decks**.

🌿 **The Spa at Constance Prince Maurice** – Known for relaxing body wraps, detox therapies, and exclusive beauty treatments.

Fine Dining: The Best Gourmet Experiences

🍽 **La Table du Château (Domaine de Labourdonnais)** – A **luxurious fine-dining restaurant** serving **authentic Mauritian-French cuisine.**

🍽 **Le Château de Bel Ombre** – Offers a **romantic dining experience in a 19th-century estate**, featuring **fresh seafood and local ingredients**.

🍽 *The Restaurant at LUX Belle Mare* – A **Michelin-recommended beachfront restaurant**, famous for its **lobster and Mauritian Creole dishes**.

For Adventure Enthusiasts: Thrills in Every Corner

Mauritius isn't just about relaxation—it's also a **paradise for adrenaline junkies**! From **scuba diving and deep-sea fishing** to **hiking through lush landscapes**, the island offers endless **thrilling activities**.

Best Adventure Activities in Mauritius

🪂 **Skydiving Over the Coastline** – Experience an **unmatched aerial view** while free-falling from **10,000 feet above the island**.

🥾 **Hiking Le Morne Brabant** – Trek through a **UNESCO World Heritage Site** with **panoramic ocean views** at the summit.

🏄 **Kitesurfing at Anse La Raie & Le Morne** – Mauritius is **one of the best kitesurfing destinations** in the world!

🤿 **Scuba Diving & Snorkeling at Blue Bay** – Explore **coral gardens, shipwrecks, and vibrant marine life** in crystal-clear waters.

🐋 **Swimming with Dolphins in Tamarin Bay** – An unforgettable **close-up encounter with wild dolphins** in their natural habitat.

🚴 **Cycling & Quad Biking at La Vallée des Couleurs** – Explore **waterfalls, lush landscapes, and the famous Seven-Colored Earth dunes**.

Final Thoughts

Mauritius is a **dream destination** that seamlessly blends **luxury and adventure**. Whether you're seeking a **private island retreat, a gourmet culinary experience, or an adrenaline-pumping activity**, this tropical paradise has something for **every kind of traveler**.

Up next, let's dive into the **rich culture and history of Mauritius**, where we explore the **island's vibrant traditions, heritage sites, and local festivals**!

Outdoor Adventures and Family-Friendly Activities in Mauritius

Mauritius isn't just a beach paradise—it's also a playground for **nature lovers, thrill-seekers, and families**. From **scenic hiking trails and world-class water sports** to **wildlife encounters and kid-friendly attractions**, the island offers **a perfect blend of adventure and relaxation**.

Whether you're looking to **explore lush forests, dive into vibrant coral reefs, or experience close-up encounters with exotic wildlife**, this chapter covers the best outdoor activities Mauritius has to offer.

Hiking Trails: Best Routes and National Parks

While Mauritius is famous for its beaches, its **hiking trails** are just as breathtaking. The island is home to **lush rainforests, volcanic peaks, and dramatic cliffs**, offering spectacular views and a chance to connect with nature. Whether you're a beginner or an experienced hiker, there's a trail for every level.

1. Le Morne Brabant (UNESCO World Heritage Site)

- **Difficulty:** Moderate to Challenging
- **Duration:** 3-4 hours
- **Highlights:**

One of the **most iconic hikes in Mauritius**, offering stunning **360-degree views** of the coastline.

Rich in **historical significance**, once serving as a refuge for runaway slaves.

Requires some climbing at the top, but the **rewarding scenery is worth it**.

2. Black River Gorges National Park

- **Difficulty:** Easy to Difficult (multiple trails available)
- **Duration:** 1–5 hours (depending on the trail)
- **Highlights:**

Mauritius' **largest national park**, covering **6,500 hectares of dense forests, waterfalls, and wildlife**.

Home to **rare bird species like the pink pigeon** and **giant fruit bats**.

Popular trails: **Macchabée Viewpoint, Parakeet Trail, and Piton de la Petite Rivière Noire** (highest peak in Mauritius).

3. Tamarind Falls (Seven Cascades)

- **Difficulty:** Moderate
- **Duration:** 2–4 hours
- **Highlights:**

A **hidden gem for waterfall lovers**, featuring **seven stunning cascades**.

Perfect for **swimming, canyoning, and photography**.

Best explored with a **local guide** to navigate tricky paths safely.

4. Pieter Both Mountain

- **Difficulty:** Challenging
- **Duration:** 3–5 hours
- **Highlights:**

Famous for its **unique rock formation shaped like a human head.**

Offers **spectacular views of Port Louis and the surrounding countryside.**

Requires climbing gear for the final ascent—best for **experienced hikers and climbers.**

Water Sports: Snorkeling, Diving, and Kitesurfing Spots

Mauritius is a **dream destination for water sports lovers**, offering **crystal-clear lagoons, coral reefs, and strong winds for kitesurfing.** Whether you're a beginner or a pro, the island has plenty of options for **underwater exploration and adrenaline-pumping activities.**

Best Snorkeling and Diving Spots

🐟 Blue Bay Marine Park (Southeast Mauritius)

- **Best for:** Snorkeling and diving

- **Why Visit?**

Protected **marine park with the most vibrant coral gardens** in Mauritius.

Home to **over 50 species of colorful fish and sea turtles.**

Perfect for **beginners, as the waters are shallow and calm.**

🌴 **Cat Island & Coin de Mire (North Coast)**

- **Best for:** Advanced diving
- **Why Visit?**

Known for **deep-sea caves, coral walls, and rich marine biodiversity.**

Frequent sightings of **reef sharks, stingrays, and barracudas.**

Ideal for those looking for an **off-the-beaten-path diving experience.**

🌴 **Île aux Cerfs (East Coast)**

- **Best for:** Snorkeling
- **Why Visit?**

A stunning island retreat with crystal-clear water and colorful marine life.

Shallow coral reefs make it ideal for families and beginners.

Plenty of restaurants and leisure facilities nearby.

Best Kitesurfing and Windsurfing Spots

Le Morne Beach (Southwest Mauritius)

- Why Visit?

One of the best kitesurfing spots in the world, with consistent trade winds.

Offers both beginner-friendly lagoons and challenging waves for experts.

Stunning backdrop of Le Morne Brabant mountain.

Anse La Raie (North Coast)

Why Visit?

Calm lagoon for beginners and a windy offshore area for advanced kitesurfers.

Less crowded than Le Morne, making it a **great spot for peaceful sessions.**

Belle Mare Beach (East Coast)

- Why Visit?

Long, white sandy beaches with perfect conditions for windsurfing.

A variety of **water sports centers offering equipment rentals and lessons.**

Wildlife Encounters: Nature Reserves and Guided Safaris

Mauritius is home to **diverse wildlife,** from **giant tortoises and deer** to **colorful birds and dolphins.** If you're a **nature** enthusiast, these reserves and sanctuaries will give you a chance to **witness rare species up close.**

1. Île aux Aigrettes Nature Reserve

Why Visit?

- A **protected sanctuary for rare birds and giant Aldabra tortoises.**
- Home to **endangered species like the Mauritius kestrel and pink pigeon.**
- **Eco-friendly guided tours** offer an educational experience.

2. Casela Nature Parks

Why Visit?

- One of the **best wildlife parks in Mauritius**, offering **safari tours, zip-lining, and animal encounters.**
- Home to **zebras, lions, giraffes, and ostriches.**
- **Unique activities** like **walking with lions and quad biking through the savanna.**

3. La Vanille Nature Park

Why Visit?

Famous for its **giant tortoises**, including **the oldest tortoise in Mauritius, aged over 100 years**!

Also features a **crocodile farm and butterfly garden**.

A great spot for **kids to learn about conservation efforts**.

4. Dolphin and Whale Watching in Tamarin Bay

Why Visit?

A **once-in-a-lifetime** chance to swim with wild dolphins.

Eco-friendly boat tours allow visitors to observe these intelligent creatures **without disturbing their natural habitat.**

Best time to go: Early morning for **dolphins**, and between July–November for **whale watching.**

For Family Travelers: Fun for All Ages

Mauritius is a **family-friendly destination**, offering **exciting activities for kids and adults alike**. Here are some of the **top attractions for families**.

🐠 **Mauritius Aquarium (Pointe aux Piments)** – A small but **interactive aquarium**, perfect for **introducing kids to marine life.**

🌴 **Botanical Garden (Pamplemousses)** – A **beautiful tropical garden** with **giant water lilies, deer, and exotic trees.**

🎢 **Splash n Fun Leisure Park (Belle Mare)** – The **biggest water park in Mauritius**, with **slides, pools, and a lazy river.**

🚂 **Sugar Museum & Factory (L'Aventure du Sucre)** – A **kid-friendly museum** with fun **sugar cane tastings and interactive exhibits.**

Final Thoughts

Whether you're hiking through **untamed landscapes, diving into the ocean, encountering rare wildlife, or making unforgettable memories with family,** Mauritius has **endless adventures waiting to be explored.** Up next, let's dive into the **island's vibrant culture, festivals, and local traditions!**

Family-Friendly and Solo Travel in Mauritius: A Comprehensive Guide

Mauritius is more than just a honeymoon destination—it's a paradise that welcomes **families, solo explorers, and adventurers of all kinds.** Whether you're traveling with children or embarking on a solo escape, this island has something to offer. From **kid-friendly resorts packed with activities** to **safe and enriching experiences for solo travelers**, this chapter will help you plan the perfect trip to Mauritius in 2025.

Kid-Friendly Resorts and Hotels

Traveling with children requires more than just a beautiful location—you need **comfort, safety, and plenty of entertainment.** Mauritius is home to **world-class family resorts** that cater to children of all ages, ensuring a **relaxing** and enjoyable stay for parents as well. Here are some of the best **kid-friendly resorts and hotels** in Mauritius.

🏠 1. Sugar Beach Mauritius (Flic-en-Flac)

Why It's Great for Families:

Kids' Club with daily activities (ages 4-11)

Babysitting services available

Large **family-friendly pools and shallow lagoons for safe swimming**

Themed entertainment nights for children

🗿 2. Long Beach Resort (Belle Mare)

Why It's Great for Families:

Spacious family suites with beachfront access

Wave Pool and Water Sports Center

Kids' and teens' clubs with **fun workshops and adventure activities**

Gourmet dining options with kids' menus

3. Constance Belle Mare Plage (Belle Mare)

Why It's Great for Families:

Complimentary snorkeling, paddleboarding, and glass-bottom boat rides

Free access to the on-site aquarium

Fully equipped kids' club with cultural and nature-based activities

Golf course for parents and mini-golf for kids

4. The Oberoi Beach Resort (Turtle Bay)

Why It's Great for Families:

Exclusive family villas with private pools

Kids' cooking and art classes

Private beach with calm, shallow waters

Personalized childcare services

Fun Family Activities: Dolphin Tours, Waterparks, and More

Mauritius offers **a variety of fun-filled activities** that the entire family can enjoy. From interactive animal experiences to **adventurous boat trips**, here are the best **family-friendly excursions**.

🐋 1. Dolphin and Whale Watching (Tamarin Bay & Black River)

Why It's a Must-Do:

A **once-in-a-lifetime experience** to see dolphins and whales in their natural habitat.

Eco-friendly boat tours allow families to enjoy **ethical wildlife viewing**.

Best Time to Visit: Dolphins (year-round, early mornings); Whales (July to November).

🎢 2. Splash N Fun Waterpark (Belle Mare)

Why It's a Must-Do:

The **largest waterpark in Mauritius** with slides, wave pools, and lazy rivers.

Designated areas for toddlers and younger kids.

On-site dining ensures an all-day experience without leaving the park.

3. L'Aventure du Sucre (Sugar Museum & Factory)

Why It's a Must-Do:

A kid-friendly museum with interactive sugar-making experiences.

Sugar tastings and chocolate pairings for the whole family.

Beautiful botanical garden and play areas for children.

4. Casela Nature Parks (West Mauritius)

Why It's a Must-Do:

Safari jeep tours to see zebras, giraffes, and lions.

Camel rides, zip-lining, and petting zoos for young children.

Quad biking and segway rides for older kids and teens.

🌴 5. Île aux Cerfs (Family Beach Day)

Why It's a Must-Do:

A **stunning island retreat** with **shallow, kid-friendly beaches.**

Water sports, mini-golf, and boat excursions for all ages.

Beachfront restaurants offering kid-friendly meals.

Tips for Traveling with Kids in Mauritius

✈ 1. Best Time to Visit with Kids

- **Avoid peak heat** (December to February) if traveling with infants or toddlers.

- **May to October** offers cooler temperatures and fewer crowds.

2. Packing Essentials

- Sunscreen, **UV-protective swimwear, and insect repellent.**
- **Travel stroller** for toddlers—some areas have uneven terrain.
- **Reusable water bottles** to stay hydrated in the tropical heat.

3. Health and Safety

- Mauritius is **safe for families**, but always use **reef-friendly sunscreen and mosquito repellent.**
- **Tap water is generally safe**, but bottled water is available everywhere.
- **Check with hotels for baby cots, high chairs, and childcare services** in advance.

4. Transportation Tips

- Renting a car is **the most flexible way to explore.**
- Public buses are available but **may not be stroller-friendly.**

- **Pre-book airport transfers** to avoid hassle upon arrival.

For Solo Travelers: Exploring Mauritius Independently

Mauritius is **one of the safest and most welcoming destinations for solo travelers.** Whether you're looking for **adventure, relaxation, or cultural immersion,** solo travelers will find **plenty of opportunities to connect with locals and explore at their own pace.**

Best Experiences for Solo Travelers

🌿 **1. Yoga and Wellness Retreats**

- Mauritius is home to **world-class wellness resorts** offering **yoga, meditation, and Ayurvedic treatments.**

- Best Retreats:

    Shanti Maurice Resort & Spa (Secluded beachfront location)

    Heritage Le Telfair Wellness Lodge (Holistic healing programs)

2. Walking Tours of Port Louis

- **Why It's a Must-Do:**

  A great way to learn about Mauritian history and culture.

  Visit **Central Market, Aapravasi Ghat (UNESCO Site), and Caudan Waterfront.**

  Street food tours allow solo travelers to enjoy local flavors safely.

3. Water Sports for Solo Adventurers

- **Le Morne** and **Belle Mare** offer lessons in kitesurfing, windsurfing, and diving.

- Solo travelers can **join group excursions** for activities like snorkeling, kayaking, and paddleboarding.

4. Cycling Through Chamarel and Grand Bassin

Why It's a Must-Do:

Explore **Mauritius' lush countryside and scenic mountains.**

Visit **tea plantations, Hindu temples, and waterfalls** along the way.

🍷 **5. Socializing in Grand Baie**

- **Best for:** Solo travelers looking to meet new people.
- **Lively nightlife, beach bars, and social events**.
- **Catamaran cruises** are great for mingling with fellow travelers.

Safety Tips for Solo Travelers

- **Mauritius is very safe**, but avoid isolated beaches at night.
- **Use ride-hailing apps** or reputable taxi services instead of flagging down random cabs.
- **Join group tours** for activities like diving and hiking for extra security.
- **Respect local customs**, especially in religious sites—dress modestly when required.

Final Thoughts

Whether you're **traveling with kids or embarking on a solo adventure**, Mauritius offers **a wealth of experiences tailored to your travel style.**

Families can enjoy **stress-free beach days, wildlife encounters, and kid-friendly resorts**, while solo travelers can **immerse themselves in local culture, thrilling activities, and wellness retreats**.

Up next, let's uncover **Mauritius' rich history, cultural festivals, and traditional experiences** to deepen your connection with this stunning island! 🌺✨

Solo And Romantic Travel In Mauritius: A Guide For 2025

Mauritius is a dream destination for all kinds of travelers, whether you're venturing alone in search of adventure or seeking a romantic retreat with your partner. This chapter explores **essential safety tips for solo travelers, ways to meet fellow explorers,** and **budget-friendly accommodations for independent journeys**. For couples, we'll dive into **luxurious honeymoon resorts, intimate experiences, and must-visit romantic locations** that make Mauritius one of the most enchanting islands in the world.

For Solo Travelers: Exploring Mauritius with Confidence

Solo travel in Mauritius is not only **safe but incredibly rewarding**. Whether you want to **hike volcanic trails, relax** on secluded beaches, or dive into the island's vibrant culture, you'll find **plenty of opportunities to connect with locals and fellow travelers** while maintaining your independence.

🛡 Safety Tips for Exploring Alone

Mauritius is **one of the safest destinations for solo travelers**, but like any place, it's important to take precautions. Here's how to ensure a **smooth and secure** solo adventure:

1. Stay in Well-Lit and Populated Areas at Night

- Mauritius is generally safe, but **avoid deserted beaches or remote areas after dark.**
- Stick to **well-populated places like Grand Baie, Port Louis, and Flic-en-Flac** if you're heading out at night.

2. Use Reputable Transportation Options

- **Ride-hailing apps like Yugo** are safer than flagging down taxis.
- If renting a car, **be cautious on winding coastal roads and drive on the left.**

- Avoid unlicensed taxis—always agree on a fare beforehand or use metered cabs.

3. Secure Your Belongings

- While crime rates are low, **keep valuables in hotel safes and avoid flashing expensive gadgets.**
- Use a **crossbody bag with a zipper** in crowded markets and tourist areas.

4. Research Before Heading Off the Beaten Path

- If hiking alone, **choose well-marked trails like Le Morne Brabant or Black River Gorges.**
- **Inform your accommodation about your plans**, especially if venturing into remote areas.

5. Respect Local Customs and Dress Modestly in Certain Areas

- While beachwear is acceptable at resorts, **dress modestly when visiting religious sites or local villages.**
- Remove shoes before entering Hindu temples and avoid taking photos of people without permission.

🥟 Social and Group Activities to Meet Fellow Travelers

Traveling solo doesn't mean you have to be alone all the time! Here are some great ways to **meet like-minded explorers and locals**:

🎴 1. Join a Catamaran Cruise to Île aux Cerfs

- A full-day cruise **with snorkeling, barbecues, and plenty of socializing**.

- Most boats **host group activities like music and games**, making it easy to meet fellow travelers.

🍜 2. Take a Mauritian Cooking Class

- Learn to prepare **authentic Creole and Indian dishes** with local chefs.

- These small-group classes **foster friendships while learning about local culture.**

3. Join a Group Hike in Black River Gorges National Park

- Connect with other nature lovers on a **guided trek through Mauritius' lush forests.**
- Guides help **navigate trails while sharing insights on native wildlife and history.**

4. Experience a Traditional Sega Night

- Head to **Flic-en-Flac or Grand Baie for a cultural evening** filled with Mauritian music and dance.
- Many beachfront restaurants **offer communal seating, making it easy to strike up conversations.**

5. Sign Up for a Surf or Diving Course

- Surf schools in **Tamarin Bay and Le Morne** welcome beginners and experienced surfers alike.
- If diving, join a **group tour to explore coral reefs, shipwrecks, and marine life.**

6. Use Travel Apps and Social Media

- Platforms like **Meetup, Couchsurfing, and Facebook travel groups** help solo travelers connect.

- Look for **local events, workshops, or meetups** happening during your visit.

🐾 Affordable Accommodations and Self-Guided Itineraries

Solo travelers often look for **affordable yet comfortable accommodations** that provide flexibility and convenience. Mauritius has **budget-friendly stays that offer great value without compromising on experience.**

🏠 Best Budget-Friendly Accommodations

1. Cosi Holiday (Flic-en-Flac)

- Affordable **beachfront apartments** with a communal vibe.
- Great for **meeting other travelers and exploring the nightlife nearby.**

2. Otentic Eco Tent (Grand River South East)

- **Glamping-style accommodation** near the river and waterfalls.
- Perfect for **nature lovers who enjoy adventure and tranquility.**

3. **Villa Narmada (Grand Baie)**

    - **Self-catering apartments** close to beaches, restaurants, and shops.
    - Ideal for solo travelers who **want independence and a central location.**

Best Self-Guided Itineraries for Solo Travelers

1. **Cultural Exploration Day (Port Louis & Pamplemousses)**

    - **Visit the Central Market** for street food and souvenirs.
    - Explore **Aapravasi Ghat (UNESCO Site)** to learn about indentured labor history.
    - Stroll through **Pamplemousses Botanical Garden.**

2. Beach-Hopping Adventure (West Coast)

- Start at **Le Morne Beach for kitesurfing.**
- Enjoy **lunch at La Gaulette with stunning ocean views.**
- End the day at **Tamarin Bay for sunset dolphin-watching.**

For Couples and Honeymooners: A Romantic Getaway in Mauritius

Mauritius is one of the **most sought-after honeymoon destinations** in the world, thanks to its **idyllic beaches, luxurious resorts, and unforgettable experiences.** Whether you're celebrating a honeymoon, anniversary, or a romantic getaway, this island is **designed for love.**

💎 Most Romantic Resorts for Couples

1. One&Only Le Saint Géran (Belle Mare)

- Private overwater cabanas with personal butler service.
- Couples-only spa treatments and sunset beach dining.

2. **LUX Grand Gaube (North Mauritius)**

- Secluded beaches and ocean-facing infinity pools.
- Candlelit dinners under the stars and couples' wellness retreats.

3. **Constance Prince Maurice (East Coast)**

- Floating overwater suites for the ultimate privacy.
- Luxury spa and helicopter rides over the island.

Unforgettable Romantic Experiences

1. Sunset Catamaran Cruise

- Sail along the **Turquoise Lagoon** with champagne and gourmet canapés.
- The **Île aux Cerfs Sunset Cruise** is a must for honeymooners.

🍽 2. Private Beach Dinner Under the Stars

- Resorts like **Shangri-La Le Touessrok** offer exclusive beachfront dining with personalized menus.

🌴 3. Couples' Spa Retreats

- Enjoy a **Mauritian coconut and sugar scrub, followed by a soothing massage**.
- Best spa resorts: **The Oberoi Mauritius & Maradiva Villas Resort**.

🚁 4. Helicopter Ride Over Mauritius

- Take in **breathtaking aerial views of waterfalls, reefs, and volcanoes**.

- Perfect for capturing **once-in-a-lifetime honeymoon memories.**

Final Thoughts

Whether you're a **solo traveler seeking adventure or a couple looking for romance**, Mauritius offers **experiences that cater to every travel style**. From **safe and social solo travel options** to **intimate and luxurious escapes for couples**, this island is a paradise waiting to be explored.

Up next, let's discover the **rich history, cultural diversity, and hidden gems of Mauritius**—unveiling the soul of this enchanting island! 🌴✨

Romantic Escapes in Mauritius: The Ultimate Guide for Couples and Budget Travelers in 2025

Mauritius is known for its **crystal-clear waters, pristine beaches, and spectacular sunsets**—making it one of the world's top destinations for **romantic getaways**. Whether you're planning a **honeymoon**, a special anniversary celebration, or just a serene vacation with your significant other, Mauritius offers a blend of **luxurious resorts, intimate beaches, and memorable activities.**

This chapter explores **romantic beach resorts, sunset cruises, honeymoon packages**, and budget-friendly options to ensure that your experience in Mauritius is unforgettable.

Romantic Beach Getaways: Resorts and Secluded Beaches

Mauritius has a collection of **luxurious beachfront resorts**, some perched on **pristine white sand beaches**, while others are nestled in **hidden coves**. Whether you're looking for seclusion or luxury, the island is **perfectly designed for couples seeking tranquility** and romance.

Top Romantic Beach Resorts

1. One&Only Le Saint Géran (Belle Mare)

- **Exclusivity at Its Best**: This iconic resort is located on a **private peninsula**, offering **unmatched privacy** with luxurious suites, each offering ocean views.

- **Romantic Activities**: Couples can indulge in **couples' massages** at the spa, enjoy **private beachfront dinners**, or take a **sunset boat ride**.

- **Why It's Special**: Known for its **elegant and spacious accommodations**, Le Saint Géran offers couples the perfect balance of **luxury and intimacy**. The resort's peaceful ambiance makes it a **top pick for romantic getaways.**

2. *LUX Belle Mare (East Coast)*

- **Beachfront Bliss**: Set along a sprawling beach, this resort is ideal for couples who want to feel **at one with the ocean.**

- **Private Villas**: Opt for the **villa experience**, complete with a private pool and butler service, offering absolute seclusion.

- **Activities for Couples**: Enjoy a **candlelit dinner by the sea**, a **couples' yoga session**, or a **private spa treatment** under the stars.

3. **The Oberoi Mauritius (Balaclava)**

- **Perfect for Romance**: Set in a **luxurious garden and beachfront area**, The Oberoi boasts some of the island's most **romantic accommodations**, including private pool villas and garden suites.

- **Dining & Experience**: Experience **private candlelight dinners on the beach** with personalized menus or take part in **cooking classes together**.

- **Why It's a Great Choice**: The Oberoi offers a perfect **balance of romance and cultural immersion**, with numerous local activities available, such as **sightseeing and guided excursions**.

Secluded Beaches: The Best Places for Intimate Moments

1. Île aux Cerfs (East Coast)

- **Private Island Vibes**: Known for its **golden sandy beaches** and **clear turquoise waters**, Île aux Cerfs is the perfect **romantic escape** for couples looking to get away from the crowds. Accessed by boat, the island offers privacy with plenty of **beachfront spots for quiet moments**.

- **What to Do**: Try a **picnic on the beach**, go snorkeling, or explore the **island's secluded coves** together.

2. Gris Gris Beach (South Coast)

- **A Secluded Sanctuary**: With **dramatic cliffs** and fewer crowds, Gris Gris is a stunning spot for couples who enjoy **solitude** and natural beauty.
- **Activities for Couples**: Perfect for a **sunset walk**, this beach offers an intimate vibe, ideal for couples seeking peace and quiet.

3. La Cuvette Beach (Grand Baie)

- **Hidden Gem**: A quiet beach with calm waters, La Cuvette is tucked away from the busy crowds of Grand Baie, making it the perfect spot for couples who enjoy privacy.
- **What to Do**: Spend the day sunbathing or take a **romantic swim in the clear waters**.

Sunset Cruises and Dinner for Two: Romantic Recommendations

Sunset cruises and romantic dinners on the beach are two of the most popular ways to celebrate love in Mauritius. These experiences offer the **perfect backdrop for intimate moments**, whether you're celebrating an anniversary, a honeymoon, or simply the beauty of Mauritius.

Sunset Cruises for Couples

1. Catamaran Cruise to Île aux Cerfs

- **Why It's Special**: Private sunset catamaran cruises are a popular choice for couples looking to take in the spectacular views of Mauritius' coastline.

- **What's Included**: A **chilled bottle of champagne**, **tropical canapés**, and the chance to swim and snorkel in crystal-clear waters.

- **The Experience**: Glide along the turquoise waters as the sun sets, casting a beautiful **orange glow across the Indian Ocean**. The ultimate way to celebrate love.

2. Dolphin Watching and Sunset Cruise (West Coast)

- **A Unique Romantic Experience**: For a truly **memorable sunset cruise**, head to the **west coast** for a combination of **dolphin-watching and an evening cruise**.

- **What's Included**: Sail with your loved one and watch the playful dolphins, then enjoy a **gourmet dinner** on board while taking in the **sunset over the ocean**.

Dinner for Two: Seaside Dining Options

1. **La Table du Château (Château Mon Désir)**

   - **Romantic Setting**: Situated in the heart of a **colonial estate**, La Table du Château offers a **beautiful dining experience** with views over the estate's **lush gardens** and the Indian Ocean.

   - **Dining Experience**: This restaurant offers an exquisite **gastronomic menu**, ideal for **intimate dinners** and romantic occasions.

2. **The Beach Restaurant (One&Only Le Saint Géran)**

   - **Private Dining**: One&Only offers a **private beachfront dining experience**, perfect for a **romantic evening under the stars**.

   - **Cuisine**: Choose from **fresh seafood and gourmet meals** prepared just for you.

   - **Romantic Vibes**: With gentle waves as the backdrop, this experience guarantees **intimacy and charm**.

Honeymoon Packages and Special Activities

Mauritius is **the ultimate honeymoon destination**, offering exclusive packages that cater to couples looking for relaxation, adventure, or both. Whether you choose to unwind in a luxurious spa or explore the island's hidden gems, there's something for every couple.

Honeymoon Packages for Every Type of Couple

1. Romantic Retreat at LUX Grand Gaube

- **Private Villas and Spa Treatments**: This package offers **luxurious overwater villas**, private dining, and personalized spa treatments, making it ideal for couples looking for **seclusion and indulgence**.
- **What's Included**: Private sunset dinners, couples' massages, and excursions to **local attractions**.

2. Overwater Experience at Constance Le Prince Maurice

- **Private Overwater Villas**: Perfect for couples who want an **exclusive experience**, this package includes **private beachfront dinners**, daily breakfasts, and **helicopter tours over Mauritius**.

- **Activities for Honeymooners**: Couples can enjoy **snorkeling, private boat tours**, and a **luxurious couple's spa day**.

For Budget Travelers: Affordable Romance in Mauritius

While Mauritius is often associated with **luxury**, it's also possible to have a romantic vacation without breaking the bank. This section provides affordable options for **budget-conscious couples** who still want to experience the best of what the island offers.

Affordable Romantic Getaways

1. **Self-Catering Apartments (Grand Baie)**

- **Why It's a Good Choice**: Renting a **self-catering apartment** allows couples to enjoy the freedom to cook together and explore at their own pace, all while **saving money** on meals and accommodations.

- **What to Do**: Visit local beaches, explore **markets**, or rent a scooter to explore the **island on your own**.

2. Budget Hotels in Flic-en-Flac

    - **Affordable Comfort**: Flic-en-Flac offers a range of **affordable hotels** and guesthouses with access to the beach and nearby attractions.

    - **How to Save**: Many accommodations offer **discounted rates for off-season bookings**, which can make your stay **both budget-friendly and romantic**.

Final Thoughts

Whether you're celebrating a **honeymoon**, an **anniversary**, or just spending quality time together, **Mauritius offers countless romantic experiences**.

From **secluded beaches and luxury resorts** to **affordable getaways** for budget-conscious couples, the island has something for everyone. Book your romantic retreat in **Mauritius in 2025**, and let the natural beauty and intimacy of this tropical paradise create unforgettable memories for you and your loved one. ■♥

Romantic Escapes in Mauritius: The Ultimate Guide for Couples and Budget Travelers in 2025

Mauritius is known for its **crystal-clear waters, pristine beaches, and spectacular sunsets**—making it one of the world's top destinations for **romantic getaways**. Whether you're planning a **honeymoon**, a special anniversary celebration, or just a serene vacation with your significant other, Mauritius offers a blend of **luxurious resorts, intimate beaches, and memorable activities**. This chapter explores **romantic beach resorts, sunset cruises, honeymoon packages**, and budget-friendly options to ensure that your experience in Mauritius is unforgettable.

Romantic Beach Getaways: Resorts and Secluded Beaches

Mauritius has a collection of **luxurious beachfront resorts**, some perched on **pristine white sand beaches**, while others are nestled in **hidden coves**. Whether you're looking for seclusion or luxury, the island is **perfectly designed for couples seeking tranquility** and romance.

Top Romantic Beach Resorts

1. One&Only Le Saint Géran (Belle Mare)

- **Exclusivity at Its Best**: This iconic resort is located on a **private peninsula**, offering **unmatched privacy** with luxurious suites, each offering ocean views.

- **Romantic Activities**: Couples can indulge in **couples' massages** at the spa, enjoy **private beachfront dinners**, or take a **sunset boat ride**.

- **Why It's Special**: Known for its **elegant and spacious accommodations**, Le Saint Géran offers couples the perfect balance of **luxury and intimacy**. The resort's peaceful ambiance makes it a **top pick for romantic getaways**.

2. *LUX Belle Mare (East Coast)*

- **Beachfront Bliss**: Set along a sprawling beach, this resort is ideal for couples who want to feel **at one with the ocean**.

- **Private Villas**: Opt for the **villa experience**, complete with a private pool and butler service, offering absolute seclusion.

- **Activities for Couples**: Enjoy a **candlelit dinner by the sea**, a **couples' yoga session**, or a **private spa treatment** under the stars.

3. **The Oberoi Mauritius (Balaclava)**

- **Perfect for Romance**: Set in a **luxurious garden and beachfront area**, The Oberoi boasts some of the island's most **romantic accommodations**, including private pool villas and garden suites.
- **Dining & Experience**: Experience **private candlelight dinners on the beach** with personalized menus or take part in **cooking classes together**.
- **Why It's a Great Choice**: The Oberoi offers a perfect **balance of romance and cultural immersion**, with numerous local activities available, such as **sightseeing and guided excursions**.

Secluded Beaches: The Best Places for Intimate Moments

1. Île aux Cerfs (East Coast)

- **Private Island Vibes**: Known for its **golden sandy beaches** and **clear turquoise waters**, Île aux Cerfs is the perfect **romantic escape** for couples looking to get away from the crowds. Accessed by boat, the island offers privacy with plenty of **beachfront spots for quiet moments**.

- **What to Do**: Try a **picnic on the beach**, go snorkeling, or explore the **island's secluded coves** together.

2. Gris Gris Beach (South Coast)

- **A Secluded Sanctuary**: With **dramatic cliffs** and fewer crowds, Gris Gris is a stunning spot for couples who enjoy **solitude** and natural beauty.

- **Activities for Couples**: Perfect for a **sunset walk**, this beach offers an intimate vibe, ideal for couples seeking peace and quiet.

3. La Cuvette Beach (Grand Baie)

- **Hidden Gem**: A quiet beach with calm waters, La Cuvette is tucked away from the busy crowds of

Grand Baie, making it the perfect spot for couples who enjoy privacy.

- **What to Do**: Spend the day sunbathing or take a romantic swim in the clear waters.

Sunset Cruises and Dinner for Two: Romantic Recommendations

Sunset cruises and romantic dinners on the beach are two of the most popular ways to celebrate love in Mauritius. These experiences offer the **perfect backdrop** for **intimate moments**, whether you're celebrating an anniversary, a honeymoon, or simply the beauty of Mauritius.

Sunset Cruises for Couples

1. **Catamaran Cruise to Île aux Cerfs**

    - **Why It's Special**: Private sunset catamaran cruises are a popular choice for couples looking to take in the spectacular views of Mauritius' coastline.

    - **What's Included**: A **chilled bottle of champagne, tropical canapés**, and the chance to swim and snorkel in crystal-clear waters.

- **The Experience**: Glide along the turquoise waters as the sun sets, casting a beautiful **orange glow across the Indian Ocean**. The ultimate way to celebrate love.

2. **Dolphin Watching and Sunset Cruise (West Coast)**

    - **A Unique Romantic Experience**: For a truly **memorable sunset cruise**, head to the **west coast** for a combination of **dolphin-watching and an evening cruise**.

    - **What's Included**: Sail with your loved one and watch the playful dolphins, then enjoy a **gourmet dinner** on board while taking in the **sunset over the ocean**.

Dinner for Two: Seaside Dining Options

1. **La Table du Château (Château Mon Désir)**

    - **Romantic Setting**: Situated in the heart of a **colonial estate**, La Table du Château offers a **beautiful dining experience** with views over the estate's **lush gardens** and the Indian Ocean.

    - **Dining Experience**: This restaurant offers an exquisite **gastronomic menu**, ideal for **intimate dinners** and romantic occasions.

2. **The Beach Restaurant (One&Only Le Saint Géran)**

- **Private Dining:** One&Only offers a **private beachfront dining experience**, perfect for a **romantic evening under the stars.**
- **Cuisine:** Choose from **fresh seafood and gourmet meals** prepared just for you.
- **Romantic Vibes:** With gentle waves as the backdrop, this experience guarantees **intimacy and charm.**

Honeymoon Packages and Special Activities

Mauritius is **the ultimate honeymoon destination**, offering exclusive packages that cater to couples looking for relaxation, adventure, or both.

Whether you choose to unwind in a luxurious spa or explore the island's hidden gems, there's something for every couple.

Honeymoon Packages for Every Type of Couple

1. Romantic Retreat at LUX Grand Gaube

- **Private Villas and Spa Treatments:** This package offers **luxurious overwater villas**, private dining, and personalized spa treatments, making it ideal for couples looking for **seclusion and indulgence.**

- **What's Included**: **Private sunset dinners**, couples' massages, and excursions to **local attractions**.

2. **Overwater Experience at Constance Le Prince Maurice**

- **Private Overwater Villas**: Perfect for couples who want an **exclusive experience**, this package includes **private beachfront dinners**, daily breakfasts, and **helicopter tours over Mauritius**.

- **Activities for Honeymooners**: Couples can enjoy **snorkeling, private boat tours**, and a **luxurious couple's spa day**.

For Budget Travelers: Affordable Romance in Mauritius

While Mauritius is often associated with **luxury**, it's also possible to have a romantic vacation without breaking the bank. This section provides affordable options for **budget-conscious couples** who still want to experience the best of what the island offers.

Affordable Romantic Getaways

1. **Self-Catering Apartments (Grand Baie)**

- **Why It's a Good Choice**: Renting a **self-catering apartment** allows couples to enjoy the freedom to cook together and explore at their own pace, all while **saving money** on meals and accommodations.

- **What to Do**: Visit local beaches, explore **markets**, or rent a scooter to explore the **island on your own**.

2. Budget Hotels in Flic-en-Flac

- **Affordable Comfort**: Flic-en-Flac offers a range of **affordable hotels** and guesthouses with access to the beach and nearby attractions.

- **How to Save**: Many accommodations offer **discounted rates for off-season bookings**, which can make your stay **both budget-friendly and romantic**.

Final Thoughts

Whether you're celebrating a **honeymoon**, an **anniversary**, or just spending quality time together, **Mauritius offers countless romantic experiences**. From **secluded beaches and luxury resorts** to **affordable getaways** for budget-conscious couples, the island has something for everyone. Book your romantic retreat in **Mauritius in 2025**, and let the natural beauty and intimacy of this tropical paradise create unforgettable memories for you and your loved one. ■♥

ACCOMMODATIONS IN MAURITIUS

Comprehensive Hotel and Resort Directory with Contact Information

Mauritius, a tropical paradise in the Indian Ocean, is renowned for its **luxurious resorts, boutique hotels,** and **affordable guesthouses**, offering accommodations that suit a wide range of preferences, budgets, and travel styles.

Whether you're looking for an extravagant getaway in a world-class resort, a cozy stay in a charming bed and breakfast, or an economical option in a guesthouse, **Mauritius has something for everyone.** In this chapter, you'll find an **extensive directory of hotels and resorts** across the island, providing essential details to help you choose the right place to stay.

Luxury Resorts: Indulge in Exquisite Comfort and Service

For travelers who want to experience the epitome of luxury, **Mauritius boasts some of the most exclusive resorts in the world.** These resorts are synonymous with **elegance, world-class service,** and **stunning ocean views.** Many are located along the island's pristine beaches, offering ultimate **privacy** and **luxury experiences**.

Top Luxury Resorts in Mauritius

1. **One&Only Le Saint Géran (Belle Mare)**
   A **legendary resort**, One&Only Le Saint Géran is a haven for those seeking **exclusivity**, impeccable service, and a **breathtaking location**. With its own private beach, 18-hole golf course, and multiple dining options, this resort guarantees an unforgettable experience.

   - **Address**: Le Saint Géran, Belle Mare, Mauritius
   - **Contact**: +230 402 2600
   - **Website**: oneandonlyresorts.com

2. **Four Seasons Resort Mauritius at Anahita (Beau Champ)**
   Known for its **spacious villas**, world-class spa, and **beautiful lagoon** views, this resort offers the perfect combination of relaxation and adventure, including water sports and golf.

   - **Address**: Anahita, Beau Champ, Mauritius

- Contact: +230 402 3100
- Website: fourseasons.com

3. **Shangri-La's Le Touessrok Resort & Spa** (Trou d'Eau Douce) This luxurious resort sits on a private island, with extensive offerings such as a **spa, fitness center, water sports**, and **fine dining**. Its tranquil atmosphere and **private beaches** make it an ideal choice for those seeking a secluded escape.

    - Address: Trou d'Eau Douce, Mauritius
    - Contact: +230 402 7400
    - Website: shangri-la.com

Mid-Range Hotels: Comfort and Convenience

For travelers who want a balance of **comfort, affordability**, and **location**, Mauritius has a wealth of mid-range hotels and resorts. These establishments provide great value, offering modern amenities, good service, and proximity to top attractions, making them perfect for couples, families, and solo travelers.

Recommended Mid-Range Hotels in Mauritius

1. *LUX Le Morne* (Le Morne) A charming, **contemporary beachfront resort**, *LUX Le Morne** combines comfort

with a natural backdrop, offering plenty of activities such as **kite surfing**, hiking, and **wellness** options.

- o Address: Le Morne, Mauritius
- o Contact: +230 401 4000
- o Website: luxresorts.com

2. **The Ravenala Attitude** (Balaclava)
A family-friendly hotel with an all-inclusive concept, **The Ravenala Attitude** is ideal for those looking to enjoy both relaxation and family fun.

The resort offers **water sports, culinary experiences**, and cultural activities.

- o Address: Balaclava, Mauritius
- o Contact: +230 204 8000
- o Website: attitude-hotels.com

3. **Veranda Paul & Virginie Hotel & Spa** (Grand Gaube)
An adults-only hotel, perfect for couples seeking a romantic and peaceful atmosphere, **Veranda Paul & Virginie** offers an intimate setting with its **spacious rooms**, tranquil spa, and **beachfront dining** options.

- o Address: Grand Gaube, Mauritius

- Contact: +230 204 1166
- Website: veranda-resorts.com

Budget-Friendly Stays: Affordable Comfort for Every Traveler

Mauritius is not just for luxury seekers—there are plenty of affordable accommodations available for those traveling on a **budget**.

Whether you prefer staying in a **guesthouse**, a **budget hotel**, or a **self-catering apartment**, Mauritius offers diverse options that allow you to experience the island without the high price tag.

Affordable Hotels and Guesthouses in Mauritius

1. **Villa Anakao** (Grand Baie) A cozy guesthouse in the lively **Grand Baie** area, **Villa Anakao** offers great value for travelers who want to stay close to the beach and local nightlife. Its **spacious rooms** and **affordable rates** make it a great budget option.
   - **Address**: Grand Baie, Mauritius
   - **Contact**: +230 263 2205

- Website: villaanakao.com

2. **Le Palmiste Resort & Spa** (Bel Ombre) Located in the peaceful area of **Bel Ombre, Le Palmiste Resort & Spa** offers an affordable stay in a tropical setting, with rooms that overlook lush gardens. The resort provides **comfortable accommodations** with access to a **spa** and **outdoor activities**.

    - **Address**: Bel Ombre, Mauritius
    - **Contact**: +230 625 5373
    - **Website**: palmistehotel.com

3. **Zilwa Attitude** (Calodyne) Situated on the northern coast of the island, **Zilwa Attitude** is a **budget-friendly resort** that offers a **local cultural experience** while providing affordable yet charming beachfront accommodation.

    - **Address**: Calodyne, Mauritius
    - **Contact**: +230 204 3800
    - **Website**: attitude-hotels.com

Self-Catering Options: Independent Travelers

If you prefer flexibility and independence, **self-catering apartments** and **holiday rentals** are perfect for your stay. Mauritius offers numerous **vacation rentals** that provide the comfort of **home** while giving you the freedom to cook your meals and explore the island at your own pace.

Self-Catering Apartments & Villas in Mauritius

1. **Mauritius Holiday Villas** (Various Locations)
   A collection of private villas scattered across the island, **Mauritius Holiday Villas** offers a variety of options from **beachfront properties** to **luxurious hideaways** in the mountains. Great for families or groups.
   - **Contact**: +230 698 9370
   - **Website**: mauritiusholidayvillas.com

2. **La Cuvette Self-Catering Apartments** (Grand Baie)
   Perfect for budget-conscious travelers who want to experience **local life**, La Cuvette Self-Catering **Apartments** are located near the beach and the vibrant **Grand Baie** area.
   - **Contact**: +230 263 4226

- Website: lacuvette.com

3. **Les Chambres d'Hotes de La Paix** (Black River)
   Offering a **comfortable stay** with self-catering facilities, this guesthouse is perfect for those who want a **budget-friendly and peaceful escape** while staying near Mauritius' southern beaches and nature reserves.

   - Contact: +230 433 2494
   - Website: chambreshotesdepaix.com

Conclusion: Finding the Right Stay for You

Mauritius offers a diverse selection of accommodations to suit every kind of traveler. From **exclusive five-star resorts** offering unparalleled luxury to **affordable guesthouses** providing a local experience, the choice is yours. By using this **comprehensive directory**, you'll have all the necessary information to book the perfect place to stay, ensuring your **Mauritian vacation** is memorable and stress-free.

CHAPTER FOUR
ACCOMMODATIONS IN MAURITIUS

Mauritius offers an eclectic range of accommodations that cater to every type of traveler, from luxurious stays in **5-star hotels** and **exclusive villas** to **budget-friendly hostels** and **charming guesthouses**. Whether you're looking for opulence, comfort, or a more affordable, authentic experience, there's a perfect place for you to rest and recharge. This chapter will guide you through the different types of accommodations available in Mauritius, providing essential details, including pricing, amenities, and contact information.

Luxury Stays: 5-Star Hotels and Exclusive Villas

Mauritius is home to some of the world's most exclusive and luxurious resorts. These **5-star hotels** and **private villas** offer unparalleled **comfort, privacy**, and **exceptional service** for guests who seek the ultimate getaway. With access to pristine beaches, state-of-the-art facilities, world-class dining, and exclusive experiences, these luxurious stays are perfect for those who want to indulge in the best the island has to offer.

Top Luxury Stays in Mauritius

1. **One&Only Le Saint Géran** (Belle Mare)

   A **legendary 5-star resort, One&Only Le Saint Géran** is known for its impeccable service and stunning beachfront location. The resort features spacious, oceanfront suites and villas, private butlers, and a wide range of high-end activities such as golf, spa treatments, and water sports.

   - **Address**: Belle Mare, Mauritius
   - **Contact**: +230 402 2600
   - **Website**: oneandonlyresorts.com

2. **Four Seasons Resort Mauritius at Anahita** (Beau Champ)

   Four Seasons is synonymous with luxury, and their **Mauritius resort** is no exception. Nestled along the edge of a tranquil lagoon, this resort offers spacious villas, a world-class spa, private pools, and dining experiences to suit every taste.

   - **Address**: Anahita, Beau Champ, Mauritius
   - **Contact**: +230 402 3100
   - **Website**: fourseasons.com

3. **Shangri-La's Le Touessrok Resort & Spa** (Trou d'Eau Douce). This exclusive resort is located on a private island and offers luxurious accommodations with magnificent ocean views. The resort features **fine dining**, an 18-hole golf course, a world-class spa, and private beach access.

    - **Address**: Trou d'Eau Douce, Mauritius
    - **Contact**: +230 402 7400
    - **Website**: shangri-la.com

Mid-Range Options: Comfortable and Affordable Hotels

For travelers who want a balance of quality and value, Mauritius offers numerous **mid-range hotels** that provide excellent service and amenities at a more affordable price. These properties typically offer comfortable rooms, great locations, and a variety of activities, making them an excellent choice for those who want to enjoy the island without breaking the bank.

Recommended Mid-Range Hotels

1. *LUX Le Morne* (Le Morne) Located on the **southern coast** of the island, *LUX Le Morne* blends **modern**

luxury with local charm. The resort is set against a backdrop of **mountain views** and **beautiful beaches**, offering guests a mix of activities such as water sports, hiking, and **wellness experiences.**

- o **Address**: Le Morne, Mauritius
- o **Contact**: +230 401 4000
- o **Website**: luxresorts.com

2. **The Ravenala Attitude** (Balaclava) A **family-friendly, all-inclusive hotel** located along the north coast of Mauritius, **The Ravenala Attitude** offers a variety of dining options, **water activities**, and cultural experiences. This is a great option for those traveling with family or friends.

- o **Address**: Balaclava, Mauritius
- o **Contact**: +230 204 8000
- o **Website**: attitude-hotels.com

3. **Veranda Paul & Virginie Hotel & Spa** (Grand Gaube) An intimate, **adults-only hotel**, **Veranda Paul & Virginie** offers an escape for couples. With its laid-back ambiance, it is the perfect destination for those seeking tranquility and quality relaxation.

- Address: Grand Gaube, Mauritius
- Contact: +230 204 1166
- Website: veranda-resorts.com

Budget-Friendly Picks: Hostels and Guesthouses

Mauritius isn't only for luxury travelers. There is a wide variety of **budget-friendly accommodations**, including **hostels, guesthouses**, and **budget hotels**. These options offer basic comforts, but they give you the chance to immerse yourself in local culture without spending too much. Perfect for solo travelers, backpackers, or families on a tight budget, these accommodations often provide a more authentic experience.

Affordable Hotels and Guesthouses

1. **Villa Anakao** (Grand Baie) A simple but comfortable guesthouse in **Grand Baie**, **Villa Anakao** offers a friendly atmosphere and is located just a short walk from the beach and local attractions.

    - Address: Grand Baie, Mauritius
    - Contact: +230 263 2205
    - Website: villaanakao.com

2. **Le Palmiste Resort & Spa** (Bel Ombre)

   Le Palmiste Resort offers a budget-conscious stay with access to outdoor pools, spacious rooms, and proximity to Mauritius' lush landscapes.

   - **Address**: Bel Ombre, Mauritius
   - **Contact**: +230 625 5373
   - **Website**: palmistehotel.com

3. **Zilwa Attitude** (Calodyne) A **budget-friendly resort**, **Zilwa Attitude** offers great value while embracing local culture. Located near some of Mauritius' most beautiful beaches, this resort offers **great family accommodations** and plenty of activities.

   - **Address**: Calodyne, Mauritius
   - **Contact**: +230 204 3800
   - **Website**: attitude-hotels.com

Unique Stays: Eco-Lodges, Boutique Hotels, and Beachfront Rentals

For those looking for a more **authentic** and **unique experience**, Mauritius offers a range of **eco-lodges, boutique hotels,** and **beachfront rentals**. These properties provide a more intimate setting, often focusing on **sustainability** and **local culture**. Eco-lodges allow you to enjoy a unique stay while reducing your carbon footprint, while boutique hotels offer a stylish and personalized experience.

Eco-Lodges and Boutique Hotels

1. **Heritage Le Telfair Golf & Wellness Resort** (Bel Ombre)

   A **boutique resort** that blends heritage charm with modern luxury, **Heritage Le Telfair** is perfect for those who want to experience the island's **natural beauty** and **Mauritian culture** in a more intimate setting.

   - **Address**: Bel Ombre, Mauritius
   - **Contact**: +230 602 9400
   - **Website**: heritageresorts.mu

2. **Riverside Eco-Lodge** (Black River) An eco-conscious lodge located in the tranquil **Black River Gorges**, **Riverside Eco-Lodge** offers a **sustainable** and **eco-friendly** retreat surrounded by nature. Perfect for nature lovers who want to enjoy a peaceful stay with a low environmental impact.

    o **Address**: Black River, Mauritius

    o **Contact**: +230 483 3457

    o **Website**: riverside-lodge.com

3. **Mauritius Beachfront Rentals** (Various Locations) Whether you want a **private villa** or a **charming beachfront apartment**, there are plenty of vacation rentals located right on the island's most beautiful beaches. Many of these rentals are **self-catering** and perfect for those who enjoy an independent stay.

    o **Contact**: +230 698 9944

    o **Website**: mauritiusbeachfront.com

Conclusion: Find the Perfect Place for Your Stay

Whether you're splurging on a **luxurious resort**, enjoying the comfort of a **mid-range hotel**, experiencing the local culture in a **budget guesthouse**, or opting for a more **unique**

eco-lodge, Mauritius offers a diverse range of accommodations to match every traveler's needs. By selecting from these options, you'll be sure to find a place that suits your style, budget, and travel goals.

CHAPTER FIVE
TRANSPORTATION AND GETTING AROUND

Mauritius, with its tropical beauty, diverse landscapes, and picturesque beaches, offers a range of transportation options for travelers. Whether you're exploring the island's bustling towns, serene beaches, or lush mountains, navigating the island is quite easy with the various transport modes available. This chapter will guide you through the most common ways to get around Mauritius, from **public buses** to **private car hires**, and offer practical tips on **cycling, walking**, and even **island hopping** by boat.

Navigating the Island: Buses, Taxis, and Car Rentals

Public Buses: Affordable and Scenic

Mauritius has a well-established **public bus system** that offers one of the most affordable ways to get around the island. The buses, run by the **National Transport Corporation (NTC)**, serve both local routes and more tourist-friendly areas, making it a great way to explore Mauritius on a budget.

- **Cost**: A typical bus ride costs around **MUR 25-40** (Mauritian Rupees), depending on the route and distance.

- **Convenience**: While buses can be **affordable**, they are not always the most convenient option for tourists, as they can be crowded and infrequent in some areas. However, major tourist destinations such as **Port Louis, Grand Baie**, and **Flic en Flac** are well-served by buses.

- **Best for**: Budget-conscious travelers, local commuters, and those looking to experience Mauritian daily life.

- **Tip**: Be prepared for limited air-conditioning on some buses, especially if you're traveling during peak hours.

Taxis: Convenient and Flexible

Taxis are a more flexible and comfortable option for those who prefer to get around Mauritius with ease. Unlike **metered taxis**, the fare is usually negotiated before the trip begins, making it essential to agree on the price in advance to avoid misunderstandings.

- **Cost**: Taxi fares in Mauritius are generally higher than bus fares, but the price depends on the destination and your negotiating skills. Expect to pay around **MUR 1,000-1,500** for short trips within towns.

- **Tip**: Always agree on the fare before getting into the taxi, as there are no meters.

- **Best for**: Travelers looking for more comfort, flexibility, and convenience. Perfect for those who want to reach remote areas or visit multiple attractions in a day.

Car Rentals: Freedom to Explore at Your Own Pace

Renting a car in Mauritius gives you the ultimate **freedom** to explore the island at your own pace. Whether you're visiting the coastal beaches or hiking through the mountains, a rental car allows you to access remote and secluded areas. Several well-established **car hire agencies** offer vehicles for daily or weekly rentals.

- **Cost**: The average cost for renting a **small economy car** starts at around **MUR 1,500-2,500** per day. Premium or 4x4 vehicles can cost significantly more.

- **Tip**: **Book in advance** to ensure availability, especially during the **high tourist season** (from December to April).

- **Best for**: Travelers who prefer flexibility and are comfortable driving on the **left side** of the road. Great for families, couples, or groups who want to explore at their own pace.

Driving in Mauritius: Rules, Tips, and Car Hire Agencies

Driving on the Left Side of the Road

In Mauritius, **driving is on the left side** of the road, which may be unfamiliar for some tourists. While driving can be easy and scenic, it's essential to stay alert, especially in **urban areas** with busy streets or winding mountain roads.

Traffic and Road Conditions

- **Traffic**: Major cities like **Port Louis** and **Grand Baie** can have **congested traffic** during rush hours, so plan your travels accordingly. However, the roads outside these areas are generally quieter and easier to navigate.

- **Road Conditions**: Main roads are **well-maintained**, though some rural areas may have **narrow** or **uneven roads**. Always drive cautiously, especially in the hills or coastal roads.

Car Hire Agencies

There are many **reliable car rental agencies** in Mauritius, offering a range of vehicles to suit different needs and budgets. Some well-known agencies include:

- **Hertz Mauritius**
    - **Contact**: +230 464 8600
    - **Website**: hertz.com
- **Europcar Mauritius**
    - **Contact**: +230 208 9999
    - **Website**: europcar.com

- **Sixt Mauritius**
    - **Contact**: +230 483 2460
    - **Website**: sixt.com
- **Best for**: Those who want the convenience of driving themselves and exploring the island independently.

Cycling and Walking Routes: Exploring on Foot or Two Wheels

Cycling Routes: Scenic Adventures

Cycling is a **fantastic way** to explore Mauritius, especially with its scenic coastal roads, charming villages, and tropical landscapes. Many cyclists enjoy biking along the coastline, through the **Sugar Cane fields**, or near **national parks**.

- **Popular Cycling Routes**:
    - **The West Coast**: Known for its **stunning views** of the **Indian Ocean**, this route includes **Flic en Flac**, **Tamarin**, and **Bel Ombre**, all great spots for biking enthusiasts.
    - **Black River Gorges National Park**: Explore the **wilderness** and **lush greenery** of the island's most famous national park.

The route is **challenging** but offers a true Mauritius adventure.

- **Rentals**: Many bike shops in **Grand Baie**, **Flic en Flac**, and **Port Louis** offer **bicycle rentals** for short or long-term use.

Walking Routes: Pedestrian-Friendly Exploration

If you're more inclined to explore on foot, Mauritius offers plenty of **walking trails** and pedestrian routes.

Popular Walking Trails:

Le Morne Brabant: This **UNESCO World Heritage Site** is one of the most iconic walking trails in Mauritius. The **moderate hike** leads to **spectacular views** over the island and the ocean.

Sir Seewoosagur Ramgoolam Botanical Garden: Located in **Pamplemousses**, this walking trail will take you through Mauritius' oldest botanical garden, home to indigenous plants and giant water lilies.

- **Tip**: Always bring **comfortable shoes**, especially for hiking or long walks.

Island Hopping: Ferries and Private Boat Services

Mauritius is not only an island but part of an **archipelago** with many smaller islands to explore. Island hopping is a must-do activity for those who want to discover more of Mauritius' hidden gems.

Ferries

Ferries are a convenient way to travel between **Mauritius** and nearby islands such as **Île aux Cerfs**, **Île d'Ambre**, and **Île aux Serpents**.

Popular Ferry Routes:

Île aux Cerfs: A stunning island perfect for **beach activities, snorkeling,** and **water sports**. Ferries depart frequently from **Trou d'Eau Douce**.

Île aux Serpents: Known for its **wilderness** and **uninhabited** nature, this island offers a peaceful escape and excellent snorkeling opportunities.

Cost: A ferry ride typically costs around **MUR 300-600** depending on the route.

Private Boat Services

For those who want a more exclusive and customizable experience, private boat services are available for **charter**. Whether you're looking for a **luxury yacht** or a **simple speedboat**, private boats are perfect for those who want to explore the offshore islands or enjoy **romantic sunset cruises**.

- **Best for**: Couples, families, or groups looking for a more personal and luxurious experience.

- **Tip**: Private boat services often include options for **fishing trips**, **snorkeling tours**, and even **beach picnics**.

Conclusion

Whether you prefer **public transportation**, a **rental car**, or the freedom of **cycling** and **walking**, getting around Mauritius is straightforward and enjoyable.

For the adventurous, **island hopping** provides an unforgettable experience. With options to suit every travel style and budget, you'll have no trouble exploring this stunning island in 2025.

CHAPTER SIX
TOP ATTRACTIONS AND THINGS TO DO

Mauritius is a true paradise for travelers seeking stunning beaches, rich culture, and breathtaking natural beauty. From its sparkling **turquoise waters** and **white sandy beaches** to its lush **mountainous landscapes** and vibrant cities, this island offers a range of attractions and activities to suit every type of traveler. Whether you're after relaxing on the beach, exploring historical sites, or immersing yourself in nature, Mauritius has something for everyone. In this chapter, we will explore some of the island's most famous and beloved beaches, including **Trou-aux-Biches**, **Flic-en-Flac**, and **Belle Mare**, along with other must-visit destinations.

Beaches of Mauritius: The Ultimate Guide

Mauritius is renowned for its **pristine beaches**, which are some of the best in the world. The island's coastline is dotted with both **popular tourist spots** and more **secluded beaches**, perfect for a wide range of activities from swimming and snorkeling to simply unwinding under the sun. Here's a breakdown of some of the most iconic beaches in Mauritius:

Trou-aux-Biches

- **Location**: Located on the **north-west coast** of the island, near the lively **Grand Baie** area, **Trou-aux-Biches** is often considered one of the most beautiful beaches in Mauritius.

- **Vibe**: This beach offers a **family-friendly atmosphere**, with its shallow, clear waters ideal for children and beginners to **snorkel**. The shoreline is lined with **palm trees** and **luxurious resorts**, creating a picturesque and relaxing environment.

- **Best For**: Snorkeling, swimming, and those looking for a quiet beach day close to shopping and dining options.

- **Things to Do:**
    - Snorkel with tropical fish at the coral reefs just off the shore.
    - Take a **boat ride** to nearby **Île aux Serpents** or **Île aux Bernaches**, perfect for a peaceful escape.

Flic-en-Flac

- **Location**: Situated on the **west coast** of Mauritius, **Flic-en-Flac** is one of the most popular beaches for both locals and tourists. It is easily accessible from the capital city, **Port Louis**, and the town of **Curepipe**.

- **Vibe**: With its wide **stretch of golden sand** and inviting **blue waters**, Flic-en-Flac is a great spot for sunbathing and swimming. It's a favorite for those who love an **active beach day** or are looking for a **lively** atmosphere in the evenings.

- **Best For**: **Sunbathing, water sports,** and watching **sunsets**.

- **Things to Do:**
    - Try your hand at **scuba diving** or **kitesurfing** with the various water sports centers along the beach.
    - Stroll along the beach at sunset for a truly magical view.

Belle Mare

- **Location:** On the **east coast** of Mauritius, **Belle Mare** beach is an absolute gem with its tranquil environment and unspoiled beauty.

- **Vibe:** Unlike the bustling beaches on the west coast, **Belle Mare** offers a more peaceful and serene atmosphere. Its long, uninterrupted stretch of sand, bordered by **luxury resorts**, makes it an ideal destination for relaxation and solitude.

- **Best For: Swimming, sunbathing,** and **romantic getaways**.

- **Things to Do:**
    - Take a morning swim or go for a **beachfront jog** along the stunning coastline.

- Enjoy a private **sunset cruise** or indulge in a **romantic dinner** at one of the upscale resorts.

Other Iconic Beaches and Coastal Areas

Le Morne Beach

- **Location**: Located at the foot of the iconic **Le Morne Brabant Mountain**, this beach is not just a paradise but also a **UNESCO World Heritage Site**.

- **Vibe**: Le Morne Beach offers the best of both worlds — **stunning views** and an opportunity for **adventurous water activities**. It's perfect for those looking to combine a relaxing day with the thrill of **windsurfing** or **kite surfing**.

- **Best For**: Water sports, hiking, and **photography**.

- **Things to Do**:
  - Hike to the top of **Le Morne Brabant** for a panoramic view of the island and its turquoise lagoons.
  - Participate in **kite surfing lessons** or enjoy a **boat ride**.

Grand Baie

- **Location**: Situated in the **north** of the island, **Grand Baie** is a lively coastal area surrounded by beautiful beaches, shopping districts, and bustling nightlife.
- **Vibe**: A popular destination for tourists who want the best of both worlds — vibrant beach vibes mixed with **modern amenities** and entertainment options.
- **Best For**: **Nightlife, shopping,** and **family activities**.
- **Things to Do**:
    - Enjoy the many **bars**, **restaurants**, and **nightclubs** that make Grand Baie famous for its vibrant nightlife.
    - Take a **glass-bottom boat tour** to see the coral reefs.

Pereybere

- **Location**: Not far from **Grand Baie**, **Pereybere** is another beautiful beach popular for its calm and clear waters.

- **Vibe**: This beach offers a relaxed vibe with a vibrant community of both locals and tourists. It's a smaller beach but offers fantastic opportunities for **snorkeling** and **swimming**.

- **Best For: Swimming, family fun, and snorkeling.**

- **Things to Do**:
  - Snorkel in the crystal-clear waters to observe vibrant marine life.
  - Visit the nearby shops and cafes for a **bite to eat** and some local shopping.

Things to Do Beyond the Beaches

While the beaches of Mauritius may steal the show, the island offers a wealth of other activities and attractions to keep you entertained throughout your stay. Whether you're a nature lover, an adventure enthusiast, or someone interested in cultural exploration, here are some of the top attractions and activities to add to your itinerary.

Black River Gorges National Park

- **Location**: In the **south-west** of the island, this national park covers over 60 square kilometers of pristine rainforest and is a must-visit for nature lovers.

- **Best For**: Hiking, **wildlife spotting**, and **bird watching**.

- **Things to Do**:
    - Hike the **Macchabee** or **Black River Peak** trails for an amazing view of the island.
    - Spot endemic species of birds and enjoy the park's waterfalls and lush landscapes.

The Botanical Gardens of Pamplemousses

- **Location**: Located near **Port Louis**, the **Sir Seewoosagur Ramgoolam Botanical Garden** is one of the oldest in the Southern Hemisphere and is home to many rare species of plants.

- **Best For**: Botanical exploration, **relaxation**, and **history**.

- **Things to Do**:
    - Explore the giant **water lilies** and **sacred lotus** in the ponds.
    - Take a guided tour to learn about the island's plant species and history.

Seven Colored Earths

- **Location**: Located in **Chamarel**, this unique geological formation features **sand dunes** of different colors — red, violet, blue, and green.

- **Best For**: Photography, **nature exploration**, and **geological wonders**.

- **Things to Do**:
    - Visit the nearby **Chamarel Waterfall** for a spectacular view of the island's landscapes.
    - Take a stroll across the **Seven Colored Earths** to admire the vibrant sands.

Conclusion

Mauritius is a destination that will captivate you with its **natural beauty**, from its **idyllic beaches** to its **lush inland landscapes**. Whether you're lounging on the soft sands of **Trou-aux-Biches**, **Flic-en-Flac**, or **Belle Mare**, or exploring the **Black River Gorges** and other national treasures, you'll find something to suit every interest. With a mix of relaxation and adventure, the island invites you to create memories that will last a lifetime.

Nature and Adventure Highlights

Mauritius is more than just a paradise of pristine beaches and luxurious resorts; it is a land of awe-inspiring **natural beauty** and thrilling **adventures**.

The island is teeming with lush landscapes, crystal-clear waters, and dramatic geological formations that make it an ideal destination for nature lovers and thrill-seekers. Whether you're into **hiking, wildlife spotting**, or exploring unique natural wonders, Mauritius offers an abundance of opportunities to immerse yourself in its natural splendor. In this chapter, we will explore some of the island's most famous nature and adventure highlights, including **Black River Gorges National Park**, the **Chamarel Waterfall**, **Seven Colored Earth**, and the renowned **Île aux Cerfs**.

Black River Gorges National Park

- **Overview**: Located in the **south-western** part of Mauritius, **Black River Gorges National Park** is a breathtaking nature reserve that covers over 60 square kilometers of tropical rainforest, rivers, and ravines. It is Mauritius's largest national park and one of the best places on the island for outdoor adventures.

Highlights:

The park is home to some of the island's **most diverse flora and fauna**, including several endemic species of birds, such as the **Mauritius Kestrel** and the **Pink Pigeon**. It's a birdwatcher's paradise.

The **rugged terrain** and dense forests make it perfect for **hiking**, with trails offering a range of difficulty levels and views that will take your breath away. The **Macchabee Trail** and **Black River Peak** are among the most popular and rewarding hikes.

The park also features several **spectacular viewpoints**, where you can see panoramic vistas of the island, including the deep ravines and lush green valleys. On clear days, the view stretches all the way to the **Indian Ocean**.

Activities:

Hiking and Trekking: Whether you're an experienced trekker or a beginner, the park has trails that suit all levels. The trails often lead to secluded areas that offer serenity and spectacular views of the island's interior.

Wildlife Watching: Explore the park and its diverse ecosystem. Keep your eyes peeled for endemic bird species, like the **Mauritius Cuckoo** or the elusive **Mauritius Fruit Bat**.

Photography: With its stunning landscapes, the park is an excellent spot for photographers looking to capture the beauty of nature.

Best Time to Visit: The park can be visited year-round, but the cooler months (April to September) offer the best hiking conditions with fewer rain showers.

Chamarel Waterfall and Seven Colored Earth

- **Chamarel Waterfall**: Located in the **south-western** region of the island, the **Chamarel Waterfall** is one of Mauritius's most iconic natural landmarks. This 100-meter-high waterfall is set against a backdrop of lush greenery and rocky cliffs, creating a dramatic scene that's perfect for photography.

Highlights:

The waterfall is located within the **Chamarel Plain**, where the **Black River Gorges National Park** meets the surrounding hills, and it can be easily reached by a short walk from the viewing platform.

Visitors can enjoy spectacular views of the waterfall cascading down into a **picturesque pool** below. The setting is ideal for a peaceful retreat or a nature walk.

The waterfall is best viewed after a **rainy season**, as the flow of water is particularly strong, creating a powerful, stunning spectacle.

- **Seven Colored Earth**: Just a short distance from the waterfall, you'll find the **Seven Colored Earth**—a natural phenomenon where the earth's surface is painted in vibrant shades of red, violet, blue, green, and brown. These **sand dunes** create a surreal landscape that is unlike anything else on the island.

Highlights:

The Seven Colored Earths are formed by the island's volcanic soil, and the colors are most vibrant after rain when the natural hues of the earth seem to shift in the light. A small lake located nearby also adds to the charm, reflecting the bright colors of the sand dunes.

Visitors can explore the area through walking paths, which allow you to appreciate the colorful landscape from different angles.

Activities:

Photography: The vibrant colors of the earth, set against the backdrop of the lush vegetation, make for extraordinary photo opportunities.

Walking and Exploration: Wander through the **Seven Colored Earths** and learn about the geological history of the island. Be sure to stop by the **nearby gift shop**, where you can purchase souvenirs and products made from the earth's unique colors.

Best Time to Visit: Early morning or late afternoon is ideal for visiting the **Chamarel Waterfall** and the **Seven Colored Earth**, as the light is softer, and the crowds tend to be smaller.

Île aux Cerfs: Day Trips and Activities

- **Overview**: Known as **Mauritius's most famous island getaway**, Île aux Cerfs is a beautiful **private island** located off the east coast of the main island. It is renowned for its **turquoise waters, white sandy** beaches, and a plethora of **water activities** that make it the perfect day trip destination.

Highlights:

The island is surrounded by a shallow lagoon, ideal for various **water sports**, including **snorkeling, scuba diving, waterskiing,** and **paragliding**.

Its pristine beaches are perfect for **relaxing**, with plenty of **sunbeds, beach bars,** and **restaurants** where you can indulge in fresh seafood while enjoying the view.

Île aux Cerfs is also famous for its **world-class golf course**, the **Île aux Cerfs Golf Club,** which is designed by renowned architect **Bernhard Langer** and offers stunning views over the Indian Ocean.

Activities:

Watersports: Try your hand at **windsurfing, snorkeling,** or **kayaking** in the crystal-clear waters around the island. You can also take a **boat tour** around the island or go on a **submarine ride** to see marine life up close.

Golf: If you're a golf enthusiast, you can spend your day on the **island's 18-hole championship golf**

course, which offers some of the best views you'll experience while teeing off.

Picnicking and Beach Days: Spend your day lounging on the beach, enjoying a delicious **picnic**, or indulging in local cuisine at one of the beachside restaurants.

- **Best Time to Visit**: The best time to visit **Île aux Cerfs** is during the dry season (April to December) when the weather is sunny, and the waters are calm, making it ideal for a range of water activities.

Conclusion

Mauritius is not just a beach destination; it is a paradise for those who want to experience the island's **stunning landscapes** and **adventurous spirit**. From hiking through the verdant trails of **Black River Gorges National Park** to marveling at the vibrant earth tones of the **Seven Colored Earth**, or exploring the pristine waters and sandbars of **Île aux Cerfs**, there is no shortage of natural wonders and thrilling activities to enjoy. Whether you are an adrenaline junkie or a nature lover, the island's diverse **adventure offerings** ensure that your time in Mauritius will be unforgettable.

Cultural and Historical Sites

Mauritius is not only known for its stunning beaches and natural beauty but also for its rich and diverse **cultural heritage**. The island's history spans centuries, influenced by various cultures and civilizations, including **Indian, African, European,** and **Chinese** communities. This fusion of cultures is reflected in the island's architecture, traditions, and way of life.

For travelers interested in **history, art,** and **local culture**, Mauritius offers a wealth of **historical sites, museums,** and **architectural gems** that provide fascinating insights into its past. In this section, we explore some of the most significant cultural and historical landmarks, including **Aapravasi Ghat, Eureka House,** and the bustling capital, **Port Louis**, with its **markets, museums,** and unique blend of **local life**.

Aapravasi Ghat: A UNESCO World Heritage Site

Overview: One of the most significant historical sites in Mauritius, **Aapravasi Ghat** is located in **Port Louis**, the capital city. This UNESCO **World Heritage Site** marks the arrival point for thousands of **indentured laborers** from India, who were brought to the island during the 19th century.

It was here that many of the island's laborers first set foot on Mauritian soil, bringing with them their culture, customs, and traditions, which have deeply influenced the island's culture today.

Highlights:

The site is a **museum** that tells the poignant story of the **Indian diaspora** and the struggles faced by the laborers who were brought to Mauritius under the British colonial rule.

Aapravasi Ghat is a **symbol of cultural heritage**, showcasing the history of the **Indian migration** to Mauritius and its impact on the island's society, economy, and culture.

The **stone structures** and **remains** of the former **immigration depot** are preserved to reflect the hardships endured by the immigrants. Visitors can explore several exhibitions that shed light on the daily lives and challenges of these workers.

Activities:

Guided Tours: Explore Aapravasi Ghat with a **local guide** who can explain the historical significance of the site and give you a deeper understanding of the cultural and social impact of the Indian laborers.

Historical Exhibits: Visit the museum housed at the site to learn more about the indentured labor system, the evolution of the Mauritian culture, and the legacy of the Indian community on the island.

Best Time to Visit: Aapravasi Ghat can be visited year-round. However, for a more immersive experience, it's ideal to go during the cooler months (May to October), when the weather is more comfortable for walking and exploring.

Eureka House: Colonial Architecture and Scenic Views

- **Overview**: The **Eureka House**, located in the heart of Mauritius in the **Moka Valley**, is one of the island's most **beautiful colonial-era buildings**. Constructed in the early 19th century, the house was once home to one of the island's wealthiest French families, and today, it offers visitors a glimpse into the grandeur and lifestyle of the island's **colonial past**.

Highlights:

The **house itself** is an exquisite example of **Mauritian colonial architecture**, featuring wide verandas, high ceilings, and traditional timber finishes.

The structure is surrounded by **lush gardens** and scenic views of the valley, making it a peaceful retreat.

Inside the house, visitors can explore a collection of **furniture** and **artifacts** that were owned by the original occupants, providing a glimpse into life during the colonial era.

The **Eureka House** is not just a historic house but also an example of the island's **multi-ethnic history**. During the years, the house served as the residence of several important figures and showcases different elements of the island's cultural evolution.

Activities:

Guided Tours: A guided tour will walk you through the rooms of the house, explaining the history of the building and its former residents. You'll hear stories about the island's colonial past and the lives of the families who lived there.

Nature Walks: The Eureka House is situated amidst picturesque surroundings, so be sure to explore the surrounding **botanical gardens** and take a leisurely walk along the **nature trails** in the area.

Tea or Lunch at the Café: The house also has a lovely **cafeteria** where you can enjoy traditional Mauritian snacks and beverages while overlooking the valley.

Best Time to Visit: The Eureka House can be visited year-round. For a quieter experience, consider visiting early in the morning or later in the afternoon, as the crowds tend to thin out, allowing you to enjoy the peaceful ambiance.

Port Louis: Markets, Museums, and Local Life

Overview: **Port Louis**, the capital of Mauritius, is the heart of the island's vibrant **local life**. The city is a **melting pot** of cultures, with an exciting mix of **traditional markets**, **colonial architecture**, and modern **commercial centers**. It's a city that's alive with activity, offering visitors a perfect mix of the old and new. Here, you can explore bustling markets, visit insightful museums, and immerse yourself in the local culture.

Highlights:

Central Market: One of the **most famous attractions** in Port Louis, the **Central Market** is a **lively and colorful marketplace** where you can shop for a variety of goods, including fresh produce, spices, textiles, and handmade crafts. It's an excellent place to witness the island's daily rhythms and pick up unique souvenirs.

Le Caudan Waterfront: This modern shopping center features a mix of **restaurants, boutiques,** and **art galleries,** giving visitors a taste of Mauritius's contemporary side. The waterfront area is also home to several **luxury hotels** and is a great place for a leisurely stroll with views over the harbor.

Aapravasi Ghat: As mentioned earlier, this UNESCO site is part of the city's rich history and one of the most significant sites in Mauritius's heritage.

National History Museum: Located in the **heart of Port Louis,** the National History Museum offers a fascinating look into the island's history, from its geological formation to its colonial past and cultural influences.

Activities:

Walking Tours: To truly experience the city, take a **walking tour** through the streets of Port Louis, exploring its **colonial buildings,** local markets, and lively neighborhoods. It's a great way to understand the blend of influences that make up the city's character.

Museum Visits: Don't miss out on a visit to the **National History Museum,** which offers a detailed perspective on the natural and cultural history of Mauritius.

Shopping: For souvenirs and local products, a stop at **Central Market** is a must. If you're after designer labels, head to the **Le Caudan Waterfront**.

- **Best Time to Visit**: Port Louis is best explored in the cooler months, especially from **April to September**. Early mornings and late afternoons are the best times to visit to avoid the midday heat and crowds.

Conclusion

Mauritius offers a diverse mix of cultural and historical experiences that will captivate history buffs, art enthusiasts, and curious travelers alike.

From the significant **Aapravasi Ghat**, which honors the history of the island's indentured laborers, to the charming **Eureka House** and the vibrant **Port Louis** with its **markets**, **museums**, and lively local scene, Mauritius has something for everyone.

These cultural gems not only offer insight into the island's past but also give visitors the chance to connect with its rich traditions and heritage. Whether you're strolling through the bustling streets of the capital, visiting historical sites, or soaking in the colonial charm, Mauritius's cultural and historical landmarks offer a unique and enriching travel experience.

Unique Experiences in Mauritius

Mauritius is a land full of **unique experiences** that allow visitors to immerse themselves in the island's rich cultural heritage, natural beauty, and artisanal traditions. While the island is renowned for its beautiful beaches and lush landscapes, there are also countless opportunities to engage in **authentic local experiences** that offer a deeper connection to the culture, history, and traditions of Mauritius. In this section, we delve into two exceptional experiences you won't want to miss: **Tea Plantation Tours** and **Rum Distillery Visits**.

Tea Plantation Tours: A Journey into Mauritius' Rich Tea Heritage

Mauritius may not be the first place that comes to mind when you think of tea, but the island boasts a centuries-old tea tradition that's tied to its **colonial past** and the influx of **Indian** and **Chinese** immigrants. **Tea plantations** have played a significant role in shaping the island's agriculture and economy, and today, they offer fascinating tours that take visitors through the **history, cultivation**, and **production** of one of Mauritius' most iconic beverages.

Overview:

Tea cultivation on the island dates back to the 18th century, introduced by the French as part of their colonial expansion. Today, **Mauritian tea** is considered a premium product, grown in the island's **highland areas** like the **Savanne District** and **Grand Bassin**. The cool, misty conditions and fertile volcanic soil make it an ideal location for producing high-quality tea leaves.

Highlights:

Visit to Tea Plantations: A typical **tea plantation tour** takes you through lush fields, where you can observe **local workers** harvesting the tea leaves by hand. Learn about the **different tea varieties**, including **black, green**, and **flavored teas**, and how they are carefully cultivated, harvested, and processed.

Tea Tasting Sessions: Many tours end with a relaxing **tea-tasting session** where you can sample various types of tea grown on the plantation. It's an opportunity to savor the **distinct flavors** of **Mauritian tea** while overlooking breathtaking views of the plantations and surrounding landscapes.

Heritage and History: As you walk through the plantation, knowledgeable guides will share fascinating insights into the island's **tea history**, explaining how tea was introduced to the island and how it became intertwined with the **island's economic development**. This makes the experience not only enjoyable but deeply informative.

Activities:

Guided Plantation Tours: Most tea plantations offer **guided tours** that take you through the entire process, from **planting** to **harvesting** to **production**. You'll gain insight into the sustainable farming practices used on the island and the important role tea plays in the local culture.

Tea Tasting: After the tour, visitors can enjoy a **tea-tasting experience**, where they'll get to sample a variety of fresh, local teas. Some plantations even offer **tea blending workshops**, allowing you to create your own custom tea blend.

Shop for Souvenirs: Don't forget to stop by the plantation's **gift shop**, where you can purchase bags of freshly packaged tea, along with **locally-made tea accessories** like teapots, cups, and tea infusers.

Best Time to Visit: Tea plantations can be visited year-round, but for the most comfortable experience, plan your visit between **May and October** when the weather is cooler and more comfortable for outdoor tours.

Rum Distillery Visits: Discover the Art of Crafting Mauritius' Famous Rum

Mauritius is also known for producing some of the finest **rum** in the world, thanks to its rich sugarcane fields that cover vast areas of the island. Rum distilleries are an essential part of the island's **agricultural heritage**, and a visit to one of these distilleries provides an authentic taste of Mauritius' culture, history, and craftsmanship.

Overview:

The origins of rum production in Mauritius go back to the early **French colonial era**, when sugarcane was introduced to the island. Today, rum is made using **local sugarcane** and a unique distillation process that has been passed down through generations. The island's rum is often enjoyed as a **refreshing cocktail base** or sipped neat for its bold, robust flavors.

Highlights:

Visit to Traditional Rum Distilleries: A visit to a **Mauritian rum distillery** offers a rare opportunity to witness the **entire rum-making process**. Tour the **sugarcane fields**, where the raw material is harvested, and learn about the various steps involved in turning sugarcane into rum, from **fermentation** to **distillation** and **aging**.

Tasting Experience: No visit to a rum distillery is complete without a **rum tasting session**. You'll have the chance to sample a variety of rum types, from **light rums** to **dark rums**, and even some of the island's signature **spiced rums**.

Many distilleries offer **tasting tours**, which include explanations of the flavors and profiles of different rums, giving you a deeper appreciation for this iconic Mauritian spirit.

Rum Cocktail Making: Some distilleries even host **rum cocktail-making workshops**, where visitors can learn how to craft cocktails using fresh ingredients and, of course, Mauritius' own rum. It's a fun and interactive way to enjoy the flavors of the island while learning the secrets behind creating perfect rum drinks.

Activities:

Guided Distillery Tours: Most rum distilleries offer **guided tours** that cover the history of rum production in Mauritius, from its origins to its present-day craft. You'll also learn about the different types of rum produced and the nuances that make Mauritius' rum so distinct.

Rum Tastings: Most tours culminate in a **rum tasting,** where you can sample the island's best rums. You'll gain insight into the **aging process** and the **flavor profiles** of the different rum varieties produced locally.

Visit the Distillery Shops: Many distilleries have onsite **shops** where you can buy locally made rum, as well as **rum-based products** such as sauces, jams, and flavored rums. It's an excellent place to pick up a souvenir or gift for those back home.

Best Time to Visit: Rum distilleries are open year-round, but the ideal time to visit is during the **cooler months** from **May to October**, when the temperatures are more comfortable for outdoor tours. During this time, you can enjoy both the distillery visit and the beautiful island weather.

Conclusion: Unforgettable Mauritius Experiences

The unique experiences of **tea plantation tours** and **rum distillery visits** provide visitors to Mauritius with a chance to discover the island's **cultural depth, agricultural heritage**, and **local craftsmanship**. These immersive activities give travelers a rare and intimate look at the island's traditions, while also offering the chance to **taste** and **experience** the flavors that are deeply embedded in Mauritian life. Whether you're sipping freshly brewed tea on a lush plantation or enjoying a carefully crafted rum at a distillery, these experiences are sure to become memorable highlights of your Mauritius journey.

CHAPTER SEVEN

CULINARY DELIGHTS OF MAURITIUS

Mauritius is a paradise for food lovers, offering a rich and diverse **culinary landscape** influenced by its **multicultural heritage**. The island's cuisine is a fusion of **Indian, Creole, French, Chinese, and African flavors**, reflecting the deep cultural history of its people. Whether you're indulging in a hearty home-cooked meal, sampling fresh seafood by the beach, or grabbing a quick bite from a street vendor, Mauritius guarantees a **delicious and unforgettable gastronomic experience**.

This chapter takes you through some of the **must-try traditional Mauritian dishes**, as well as the **best places to experience authentic street food and local market delights**.

Traditional Mauritian Dishes You Must Try

Mauritian cuisine is a perfect blend of **spices, fresh ingredients, and unique cooking techniques**, giving each dish its own distinct character. Here are some of the **most iconic traditional dishes** you shouldn't miss when visiting Mauritius:

Dholl Puri – The National Street Food of Mauritius

One of the most **beloved street foods** in Mauritius, Dholl Puri is a **soft, thin, yellow split-pea flatbread** served with a variety of delicious fillings. It is typically accompanied by **rougaille (a rich tomato-based sauce), bean curry, and a side of pickles or chutney**.

- **Where to Try It:**
    - **Dewa & Sons** (Port Louis) – One of the most famous places for Dholl Puri.
    - **Rose Hill Market** – A great spot for authentic, locally made versions.

Bol Renversé (Upside-Down Bowl)

A unique and flavorful dish of **stir-fried vegetables, chicken or seafood, and a rich, thick sauce** poured over **steamed rice and topped with a fried egg**. It is then flipped onto a plate, creating a visually appealing and mouthwatering meal.

Where to Try It:

Dragon Vert (Quatre Bornes) – Known for its delicious Chinese-Mauritian dishes.

Tien Fai Garden (Port Louis) – A great place to experience authentic Bol Renversé.

Rougaille – A Staple of Mauritian Cuisine

Rougaille is a **tomato-based Creole stew** flavored with **garlic, onions, thyme, and chilies**. It is often served with **fish, prawns, sausages, chicken, or even paneer** for a vegetarian option. This dish is a staple in Mauritian households and pairs well with **rice or bread**.

Where to Try It:

> **Le Chamarel Restaurant** – Offers a scenic view while enjoying an authentic plate of Rougaille.
>
> **Chez Tante Athalie** – A charming spot with a home-cooked Creole menu.

Mine Frit (Mauritian Fried Noodles)

A Chinese-inspired dish, Mine Frit consists of **wok-fried noodles with vegetables, eggs, chicken, or seafood**, tossed with soy sauce and sometimes topped with a fried egg. This is one of the most **popular comfort foods** on the island.

Where to Try It:

> **China Town (Port Louis)** – The best place to find an authentic plate of Mine Frit.
>
> **Ti Kouloir** – Famous for its flavorful Mauritian-Chinese dishes.

Boulettes (Mauritian Dumplings)

Inspired by Chinese cuisine, Boulettes are **steamed dumplings made of fish, chicken, or vegetables**. These dumplings are often served in a **light broth** and are incredibly popular among locals.

Where to Try It:

- **Port Louis' Chinatown** – The best place to experience traditional Boulettes.
- **First Restaurant (Quatre Bornes)** – A local favorite for a hearty bowl of dumplings.

Octopus Curry (Cari Ourite)

Mauritian curries are rich, fragrant, and filled with spices, and one of the island's **most iconic** versions is Octopus Curry. Fresh **octopus is slow-cooked with turmeric, garlic, onions, and tomatoes**, creating a tender and flavorful dish best enjoyed with **rice or farata (a local flatbread)**.

Where to Try It:

- **Chez Rosy (Gris Gris)** – Serves one of the best Octopus Curries on the island.
- **La Case du Pecheur** – A great spot for seafood lovers.

Farata (Mauritian Roti)

A popular **Indian-inspired flatbread**, Farata is usually served with **curries, rougaille, or pickles**. This flaky and soft bread is a staple in Mauritian cuisine and is often sold as **a quick snack at street stalls**.

Where to Try It:

> **Bazaar Port Louis** – Plenty of vendors selling fresh Faratas.
>
> **Grand Baie Market** – A great spot for street food lovers.

Street Food Hotspots and Local Markets

One of the best ways to **experience authentic Mauritian cuisine** is by exploring the island's **street food culture** and vibrant local markets. These places offer an explosion of flavors, aromas, and colors, making them a paradise for food lovers.

Best Street Food Hotspots

Port Louis Central Market

> Located in the heart of the capital, this bustling market is a **must-visit** for food lovers.
>
> Try **Dholl Puri, Gateaux Piments (chili cakes), and Alouda (a sweet vanilla-flavored milk drink).**

Mahebourg Waterfront Street Food Stalls

> A **seaside setting** offering an array of delicious street food.

Try **Fish Vindaye, Chilli Bites, and local Mauritian sausages.**

Grand Baie Night Market

A great place for **fresh seafood, grilled meats, and fried snacks.**

Best for **Mine Frit, Boulettes, and Farata wraps.**

Flic-en-Flac Beach Street Vendors

Enjoy street food with a view of the beach.

Try **fresh coconut water, samosas, and fresh tropical fruit.**

Best Local Markets for Fresh Ingredients and Spices

1. **Flacq Market** – The **largest open-air market** in Mauritius, perfect for buying fresh vegetables, exotic spices, and local street food.
2. **Goodlands Market** – Best known for its **variety of fresh seafood and tropical fruits.**
3. **Quatre Bornes Market** – Famous for its **spice stalls** and authentic Mauritian condiments.

Final Thoughts

Mauritian cuisine is an **exciting blend of flavors and cultures**, offering something for every taste. Whether you're sitting at a beachside restaurant, exploring a bustling food market, or grabbing a quick bite from a local food stall, the island's **rich culinary heritage** is something that will stay with you long after your trip.

From **savory street food favorites like Dholl Puri and Farata** to **hearty meals like Rougaille and Octopus Curry**, there's no shortage of delicious dishes to discover in Mauritius. Be sure to **venture beyond the tourist spots** and explore **local eateries and street food stalls** to get a true taste of the island's vibrant food scene.

No trip to Mauritius is complete without **indulging in its incredible cuisine**, so grab a plate, dig in, and enjoy the **flavors of paradise!**

Fine Dining and Culinary Experiences in Mauritius

Mauritius is not only a paradise of **pristine beaches, lush landscapes, and rich cultural heritage** but also a destination that boasts an impressive **culinary scene**. The island is home to **world-class fine dining restaurants**, innovative chefs, and unique gastronomic experiences that cater to every palate, including **vegetarian, vegan, and gluten-free travelers.**

Whether you're looking for a **Michelin-worthy gourmet experience, a plant-based feast, or an interactive cooking class,** Mauritius has something exceptional to offer. This chapter explores the **best fine dining restaurants, specialty dietary options, and immersive food tours** that will elevate your culinary adventure on the island.

Fine Dining Restaurants for Gourmet Lovers

Mauritius has no shortage of **luxurious dining establishments,** many of which are located within **prestigious resorts and boutique hotels.** These restaurants offer exquisite menus that blend **French, Creole, Indian, and Asian influences,** often using **locally sourced ingredients and fresh seafood.**

Here are some of the best **fine dining restaurants in Mauritius** that every food enthusiast should experience:

Château Mon Désir (Balaclava) – French and Mauritian Gastronomy

- Located in an elegant **colonial-style mansion,** this award-winning restaurant offers a **sophisticated blend of French and Mauritian cuisine.**

- The **Sunday brunch** overlooking the historical ruins of Balaclava is a must.
- Signature Dish: **Lobster Bisque, Duck Confit, and Vanilla Soufflé.**

La Table du Château (Domaine de Labourdonnais) – Fine Dining in a Historic Setting

- A **picturesque estate restaurant** set within a restored château, offering a menu inspired by **seasonal, locally sourced ingredients.**
- A perfect choice for **romantic dinners or special occasions.**
- Signature Dish: **Mauritian Venison Stew with Mashed Breadfruit.**

The Test Kitchen (Tamarin Bay) – A Multi-Course Culinary Journey

- Helmed by **British-South African chef Luke Dale-Roberts**, this restaurant is known for its **innovative tasting menus** that push the boundaries of Mauritian cuisine.
- Signature Dish: **Curried Octopus with Coconut Foam.**

Amari by Vineet (Four Seasons Resort) – Contemporary Indian Cuisine

- Michelin-starred chef **Vineet Bhatia** brings modern Indian flavors to Mauritius, using **locally sourced seafood, spices, and produce.**
- Signature Dish: **Tandoori Prawns with Mango Chutney.**

Le Château de Bel Ombre (Heritage Le Telfair) – Elegant French-Mauritian Fusion

- Dine in a **19th-century colonial mansion** surrounded by lush gardens.
- Signature Dish: **Grilled Red Snapper with Vanilla Butter Sauce.**

Stars Restaurant (Shanti Maurice Resort) – Oceanfront Gourmet Dining

- Known for its **stunning sea views** and **exceptional seafood dishes**.
- Signature Dish: **Mauritian Bouillabaisse with Fresh Lobster**.

Le Fangourin (L'Aventure du Sucre) – A Gourmet Sugar Estate Experience

- Located within a former **sugar plantation**, this restaurant offers **authentic Creole dishes with a gourmet twist**.
- Signature Dish: **Grilled Pineapple with Spiced Rum Glaze**.

Vegetarian, Vegan, and Gluten-Free Options in Mauritius

Mauritius is a **fantastic destination for plant-based and gluten-free travelers,** thanks to its **diverse culinary influences** and abundance of **fresh tropical produce, legumes, and grains**. Many restaurants, including street food vendors, cater to **vegetarian, vegan, and gluten-free** diets with delicious options that don't compromise on flavor.

Best Vegetarian and Vegan Restaurants

Lakaz Cascavelle (Flic-en-Flac) – 100% Plant-Based Gourmet Cuisine

- A fully vegan restaurant serving creative dishes like **Jackfruit Curry, Beetroot Carpaccio, and Vegan Cheesecakes.**

Green Spoon (Grand Baie) – Health-Conscious and Organic

- Specializes in **organic, gluten-free, and vegan-friendly dishes,** including **quinoa bowls, smoothie bowls, and raw desserts.**

Vida e Caffè (Multiple Locations) – Vegan Breakfast & Coffee Spot

- Offers **plant-based lattes, avocado toasts, and smoothie bowls.**

Mystic Masala (Port Louis) – Authentic Indian Vegetarian Cuisine

- A paradise for **vegetarian lovers,** offering dishes like **Paneer Tikka, Dosa, and Dal Tadka.**

Nourish by The Bay (Pereybere) – Eco-Friendly Vegan Café

- A **beachside** spot with a menu focused on sustainable, organic, and plant-based dishes.

Gluten-Free Friendly Restaurants

- **Kogi Kogi (Trou aux Biches)** – Offers gluten-free sushi and rice-based dishes.
- **Beach Rouge (LUX Grand Baie)** – Serves gluten-free pasta and fresh seafood.
- **Escale Créole (Moka)** – Specializes in **Creole** gluten-free curries and stews.

Food Tours and Cooking Classes – Immersive Culinary Experiences

For those who want to go beyond just eating and truly **immerse themselves in Mauritian cuisine**, food tours and cooking classes are an incredible way to discover the island's **culinary heritage, local ingredients, and cooking techniques**.

Best Food Tours in Mauritius

Port Louis Street Food Tour

- Explore the capital's bustling streets while sampling **Dholl Puri, Gateaux Piments, and Alouda.**

Flacq Market Food Walk

- A guided tour through one of the **biggest open-air markets,** tasting **fresh tropical fruits, seafood snacks,** and homemade pickles.

Tea and Spice Trail Tour

- Visit **tea plantations and spice gardens,** learning about **vanilla, cinnamon, and locally grown herbs.**

Best Cooking Classes in Mauritius

Mauritian Creole Cooking Class (Labourdonnais)

- Learn to prepare **traditional Creole dishes** like Rougaille, Cari Ourite, and Chutneys.

Vegan Cooking Workshop (Grand Baie)

- A plant-based cooking experience using **local fruits, vegetables, and spices.**

Seafood Masterclass (Le Morne)

- Hands-on experience in preparing **grilled fish, seafood curries, and octopus salad.**

Final Thoughts

Mauritius is an **undisputed paradise for food lovers**, whether you're indulging in a **gourmet fine-dining experience, enjoying a plant-based meal, or learning to cook traditional dishes.** The island offers **a diverse culinary landscape**, ensuring that every traveler—**whether a meat lover, vegetarian, or gluten-free diner**—can experience the best of its flavors.

To truly savor Mauritius, don't just **taste** its food—**immerse yourself in it** by exploring **local markets, joining cooking classes, and discovering the island's rich food culture.** Wherever your culinary journey takes you, Mauritius promises an unforgettable gastronomic adventure!

CHAPTER EIGHT
SHOPPING IN MAURITIUS

Shopping in Mauritius is more than just a retail experience—it's an **adventure that blends culture, craftsmanship, and luxury**. Whether you're browsing lively street markets for **handmade souvenirs**, exploring elegant **boutique stores**, or taking advantage of **duty-free deals**, Mauritius has something for every shopper.

From intricately woven **handicrafts and locally designed fashion** to **high-end jewelry and tax-free electronics**, shopping in Mauritius offers both **authenticity and affordability**. To help you make the most of your retail experience, this chapter will guide you through the best **markets, duty-free shops, and designer boutiques**, while also providing practical **bargaining tips** to ensure you get the best value for your money.

Local Markets: Where to Find Handmade Crafts and Souvenirs

For an **authentic Mauritian shopping experience**, visiting the island's **vibrant local markets** is a must. These markets are full of **color, culture, and creativity**, offering everything from **handwoven baskets and wooden sculptures to exotic spices and hand-dyed textiles**.

Best Local Markets for Authentic Souvenirs

Port Louis Central Market (Bazaar of Port Louis)

- The **oldest and most famous** market in Mauritius.
- A great place to buy **local spices, herbal teas, handmade jewelry, and traditional clothing**.
- Don't miss the **wooden model ships**, which are handcrafted with precision.

Mahebourg Market (Monday Market)

- A **bustling open-air market** that operates every Monday.
- Known for **handwoven bags, straw hats, and Mauritian street food** like dholl puri.
- Ideal for travelers looking for **budget-friendly souvenirs**.

Flacq Market

- The **largest open-air market** in Mauritius.
- Offers a wide range of **handmade textiles, embroidered scarves, and beaded jewelry**.
- Great place to **buy fresh local fruits and artisanal jams**.

Grand Baie Bazaar

- A favorite among tourists looking for **custom-made souvenirs and local artwork.**
- Features boutique stalls selling **hand-painted ceramics, colorful beach sarongs, and rattan home decor.**

Goodlands Market

- Best known for **handwoven baskets, cane furniture, and handcrafted wooden sculptures.**
- A great spot to buy **local rum-infused chocolates and homemade Mauritian pickles.**

Duty-Free Shopping: Best Deals on Jewelry, Electronics, and Perfumes

Mauritius is one of the best places in the Indian Ocean for **duty-free shopping,** offering visitors significant savings on **luxury goods** such as **watches, designer perfumes, and high-end jewelry.** The island is home to **several duty-free malls and boutiques,** making it a hotspot for those looking for **premium products at tax-free prices.**

Where to Find the Best Duty-Free Deals

Bagatelle Mall (Moka)

- The largest **shopping complex** in Mauritius.
- Features international brands such as **MAC, Hugo Boss, Lacoste, and Swarovski.**

- Offers duty-free deals on **perfumes, cosmetics, and watches.**

Le Caudan Waterfront Duty-Free Shops (Port Louis)

- A shopping hub with **luxury boutiques and jewelry stores.**
- Great for tax-free **gold and diamond jewelry, designer sunglasses, and fragrances.**

- Houses the famous **Shibani Jewels and Adamas Fine Jewelry** stores.

Mauritius Duty-Free Paradise (SSR International Airport)

- The best spot for last-minute **tax-free shopping** before your departure.
- Offers discounts on **whisky, rum, cigars, and branded skincare products**.

Ravior Jewelry (Quatre Bornes)

- One of the most prestigious **jewelry designers** in Mauritius.
- Specializes in **gold, platinum, and gemstone pieces inspired by Mauritian culture**.

Grand Baie La Croisette

- A **modern shopping destination** featuring luxury fashion, tech gadgets, and duty-free accessories.
- Home to boutiques selling **Mauritian designer fashion and premium watches**.

Boutique Stores: Fashion, Home Decor, and Art Pieces

Beyond markets and malls, Mauritius has a growing scene of **high-end boutique stores** that cater to **fashion lovers, home** decor enthusiasts, and art collectors. Many local designers incorporate **Mauritian motifs, natural materials, and island-inspired aesthetics** into their work, making these pieces one-of-a-kind.

Top Boutique Stores in Mauritius

Island Haze (Fashion & Beachwear)

- Known for its **trendy beachwear, swimsuits, and island-style casual clothing.**
- Offers a wide range of **tropical prints and lightweight fabrics** perfect for the Mauritian climate.

Colors & Sense (Home Decor & Gifts)

- Specializes in **handmade candles, decorative cushions, and wood-carved home accessories.**
- A great place to buy **eco-friendly souvenirs** made from recycled materials.

Poncini (Luxury Watches & Jewelry)

- A renowned jewelry store selling **Swiss watches, diamonds, and fine jewelry.**
- Known for its **custom-made engagement rings** with locally sourced gemstones.

Maniglier Gallery (Fine Art & Paintings)

- Features the artwork of **Alain Maniglier, a celebrated French-Mauritian artist.**
- Offers stunning **island-inspired paintings** and **limited-edition prints.**

The Shell Gallery (Handmade Crafts)

- A specialty store dedicated to **handcrafted seashell art, coral jewelry, and marine-themed decor.**
- Ideal for collectors and those looking for **ocean-inspired souvenirs.**

Tips for Bargaining and Avoiding Tourist Traps

While shopping in **local markets and small boutiques**, knowing how to **negotiate prices** and **spot genuine products** can help you get the best deals while avoiding overpriced tourist traps.

Bargaining Tips for Local Markets

✔ **Start Low, But Be Respectful** – Begin by offering **half the asking price** and slowly work towards a fair middle ground.

✔ **Buy in Bulk for Discounts** – Vendors are more likely to lower prices if you purchase **multiple items.**

✔ **Compare Prices Before Committing** – Walk around and check prices at different stalls before making a purchase.

✔ **Show Interest, But Don't Seem Desperate** – If you appear too eager, sellers may not be willing to negotiate.

✔ **Use Cash Instead of Cards** – Many markets prefer **cash transactions**, and vendors may offer discounts for cash payments.

How to Avoid Tourist Traps

✘ **Avoid Overpriced "Authentic" Handicrafts** – Some stalls sell **mass-produced souvenirs** disguised as **handmade items**. Look for artisans who are actually crafting their pieces on-site.

✘ **Beware of Inflated Prices in Resort Gift Shops** – While convenient, resort shops often sell **souvenirs and crafts at double or triple the market price**.

✘ **Watch Out for Fake Branded Items** – Some vendors sell **counterfeit watches, handbags, and perfumes**, so be cautious when buying designer goods from street stalls.

✘ **Don't Get Pressured Into Buying** – Some sellers can be **persistent**, but it's okay to walk away if you're not comfortable with the price.

Final Thoughts

Shopping in Mauritius is an **exciting experience that goes beyond retail therapy**—it's a way to connect with **local artisans, discover island traditions, and take home a piece of Mauritius**. Whether you're **bargaining for handcrafted souvenirs, indulging in duty-free luxury, or browsing boutique designer stores**, there's something special for every traveler.

By exploring **local markets, high-end shops, and art galleries**, you'll find **meaningful keepsakes** that serve as lasting memories of your journey to this tropical paradise. Happy shopping!

CHAPTER NINE
OUTDOOR ADVENTURES AND ACTIVITIES

Mauritius, often celebrated for its pristine beaches and luxury resorts, is also a paradise for **outdoor enthusiasts** seeking thrilling adventures. Whether you prefer **hiking through lush landscapes, exploring the vibrant marine world, or encountering majestic dolphins**, the island offers a **perfect blend of land and sea activities.**

From the iconic **Le Morne Brabant hike**, which rewards climbers with breathtaking views, to the **crystal-clear waters teeming with marine life**, every corner of Mauritius invites exploration. Whether you're an adrenaline junkie or a nature lover, this chapter will guide you through **the best hiking trails, exhilarating marine adventures, and unforgettable outdoor experiences.**

Hiking Trails: Le Morne Brabant and Other Scenic Routes

Mauritius is home to **diverse hiking trails** that take you through **forests, mountains, waterfalls, and coastal cliffs.** While some trails offer **leisurely nature walks**, others challenge adventurers with **steep climbs and rugged terrain.**

Le Morne Brabant – The Legendary Hike

📍 **Location:** Southwest Mauritius
⏳ **Duration:** 3-4 hours round trip
⚫ **Difficulty:** Moderate to challenging
⭐ **Best for:** Panoramic views, history, and adventure

Le Morne Brabant is the **most famous hiking trail in Mauritius** and a **UNESCO World Heritage Site**. Rising **556 meters above sea level**, this mountain is **steeped in history**, once serving as a refuge for **escaped slaves in the 18th and 19th centuries**. Today, it stands as a symbol of **freedom and resilience**, attracting hikers from around the world.

Highlights of the Le Morne Brabant Hike:

- The trail begins **through lush vegetation**, where you may spot **tropical birds and wildflowers.**

- As you ascend, the path gets **steeper and more challenging**, requiring **good stamina and sturdy footwear.**

- At the summit, you'll be rewarded with a **breathtaking 360-degree view** of the **turquoise lagoon, coral reefs, and lush forests.**

- **Best time to hike:** Early morning for cooler temperatures and stunning sunrise views.

🔴 **Safety Tip:** The final stretch is **steep and rocky**, so if you're not comfortable with heights, consider stopping at the **viewpoint just before the summit**.

Other Scenic Hiking Trails in Mauritius

1. Black River Gorges National Park

📍 **Location:** Southwest Mauritius

⏳ **Duration:** 2-5 hours (depending on the trail)

🔴 **Difficulty:** Easy to challenging

⭐ **Best for:** Nature lovers, birdwatchers, and waterfall seekers

The **largest national park in Mauritius**, Black River Gorges is a haven for **hiking and wildlife spotting**. The park features **multiple trails**, leading to **stunning waterfalls, dense forests, and panoramic viewpoints**.

- **Popular trails:** Macchabée Trail, Gorges Viewpoint Trail, and Alexandra Falls Trail.

- **Wildlife spotting:** Keep an eye out for the rare Mauritius kestrel, echo parakeet, and pink pigeon.
- **Waterfalls:** Tamarind Falls (7 Cascades) is a must-visit for those who love **cascading waterfalls and natural pools**.

2. Tamarind Falls (7 Cascades) Hike

📍 **Location:** Near Henrietta village
⏳ **Duration:** 3-4 hours
⚫ **Difficulty:** Moderate
⭐ **Best for:** Waterfall lovers and adventure seekers

This **spectacular hike** takes you to **seven cascading waterfalls**, where you can **swim in natural pools, abseil down rocks, and explore hidden lagoons**.

3. Lion Mountain Trail

📍 **Location:** Southeast Mauritius
⏳ **Duration:** 2-3 hours
⚫ **Difficulty:** Moderate
⭐ **Best for:** Stunning Ocean views

Named for its **lion-shaped silhouette**, this mountain offers **stunning views of the island's southeast coast** and the **Île aux Aigrettes nature reserve**.

4. Signal Mountain

- **Location:** Near Port Louis
- **Duration:** 1-2 hours
- **Difficulty:** Easy
- **Best for:** Cityscape views

A **short and easy hike** leading to **panoramic views of Port Louis and the coastline**, ideal for those looking for a **quick outdoor escape**.

Marine Adventures: Scuba Diving, Snorkeling, and Dolphin Watching

Mauritius is **renowned for its vibrant marine life**, with warm waters, **stunning coral reefs, and diverse underwater ecosystems**. Whether you prefer **deep-sea diving, shallow snorkeling, or dolphin encounters**, the island offers **world-class marine experiences**.

Scuba Diving in Mauritius

Mauritius is a **dream destination for scuba divers**, boasting **crystal-clear waters, shipwrecks, and colorful coral gardens**.

Best Dive Sites in Mauritius:

🍷 **Blue Bay Marine Park** – Famous for its **coral reefs and diverse fish species.**

🍷 **Cathedral (Flic en Flac)** – A dramatic underwater cave system with **majestic rock formations.**

🍷 **Coin de Mire** – Great for **beginner and advanced divers,** with **clear waters and abundant marine life.**

🍷 **St. Jacques Passage** – Home to **rays, reef sharks, and stunning coral walls.**

■ **Best time for diving:** October to April for the clearest visibility.

Snorkeling: Discovering the Coral Reefs

For those who prefer to stay closer to the surface, **snorkeling in Mauritius** offers an equally mesmerizing experience. Many lagoons are **shallow and teeming with marine life**, making it ideal for families and beginners.

Top Snorkeling Spots:

- **Blue Bay Marine Park** – One of the **best snorkeling locations**, with **crystal-clear waters and vibrant coral gardens**.

- **Île aux Cerfs** – A picturesque island with **shallow reefs and colorful fish**.

- **Pointe aux Piments** – Known for **sea turtles and tropical fish**.

- **Trou aux Biches** – Offers **calm, clear waters perfect for beginners**.

■ **Best time for snorkeling:** Year-round, but conditions are best from **October to May**.

Dolphin Watching and Swimming

One of the **most magical experiences** in Mauritius is the opportunity to **see dolphins in their natural habitat**. The waters around the island are home to **bottlenose and** spinner dolphins, which can often be spotted **swimming and playing in pods.**

Where to Spot Dolphins in Mauritius:

🐬 **Tamarin Bay** – The most famous spot for **early morning dolphin watching.**

🐬 **Black River & Flic en Flac** – Offers a **high chance of spotting dolphins** and even whales (during the migration season).

■ **Best time for dolphin watching:** Early morning between **6 AM and 9 AM** when dolphins are most active.

🌿 **Ethical Tip:** Choose **responsible tour operators** who follow guidelines to **avoid disturbing the dolphins.** Avoid tours that **chase or corner the animals,** as this disrupts their natural behavior.

Final Thoughts

Mauritius is not just about **beaches and resorts**—it's a playground for **adventure seekers and nature lovers.** From the **breathtaking summit of Le Morne Brabant** to the **thriving underwater world of Blue Bay Marine Park,** every activity allows you to experience **the island's raw beauty** in a unique way.

Whether you're **hiking through lush forests, diving alongside tropical fish, or watching dolphins at sunrise**, Mauritius promises **unforgettable outdoor adventures** that will leave you in awe. So lace up your boots, grab your snorkel, and get ready to explore the wild side of Mauritius!

CHAPTER TEN
OUTDOOR ADVENTURES IN MAURITIUS:

Water Sports, Deep-Sea Fishing & Golf

Mauritius is a paradise for outdoor enthusiasts, offering a perfect blend of **thrilling water sports, world-class deep-sea fishing, and top-tier golf courses.** Whether you're chasing the wind on a kitesurf, casting a fishing line into the deep blue, or enjoying a leisurely round of golf against a backdrop of volcanic mountains and turquoise lagoons, Mauritius delivers **exceptional experiences for every traveler.**

This chapter dives deep into **the best water sports locations, essential tips for deep-sea fishing, and the top golf courses where you can tee off in style.**

Water Sports: Kitesurfing, Windsurfing, and Paddleboarding

The warm waters and steady trade winds make Mauritius one of the **best destinations in the world for water sports.** Whether you're a seasoned pro or an eager beginner, you'll find a variety of **kitesurfing, windsurfing, and paddleboarding spots** suited to all skill levels.

Kitesurfing in Mauritius: Ride the Wind and Waves

Mauritius is a **global hotspot for kitesurfing**, thanks to its **consistent wind conditions, large lagoons, and reef-protected waters**. The south and west coasts are particularly popular, with **Le Morne being one of the best kitesurfing locations on the planet**.

Best Kitesurfing Spots in Mauritius:

🪁 **Le Morne** – The ultimate kitesurfing destination with **flat-water lagoons for beginners** and **strong waves for experts**.

🪁 **Belle Mare** – Ideal for **beginners**, with shallow waters and moderate winds.

🏄 **Anse la Raie** – Perfect for **freestyle kitesurfing** due to its steady winds.

🏄 **Pointe d'Esny** – A beautiful, uncrowded spot great for **long kitesurfing sessions**.

🔲 **Best time for kitesurfing:** June to October (strongest winds).

Pro Tip: If you're new to kitesurfing, **book lessons with certified instructors**. Many schools, especially in **Le Morne**, offer courses for beginners.

Windsurfing: Master the Indian Ocean Breeze

Mauritius offers **ideal conditions for windsurfing**, with steady trade winds and warm waters year-round. Windsurfing is **less extreme than kitesurfing** but still provides an exciting ride across the lagoons.

Top Windsurfing Locations:

🏄 **Le Morne** – Great for both **freestyle and wave windsurfing**.

🏄 **Bel Ombre** – A favorite among advanced windsurfers for **its strong waves**.

🏄 **Pointe d'Esny & Blue Bay** – Best for **calmer conditions and learning the basics**.

■ **Best time for windsurfing:** June to October (peak trade winds).

Paddleboarding: A Serene Exploration of the Lagoons

For those who prefer a more **relaxed water activity**, stand-up paddleboarding (SUP) is a great way to **explore the coastline and mangrove forests** at your own pace. The **calm lagoons and clear waters** make Mauritius an excellent destination for paddleboarding.

Top Paddleboarding Locations:

🏄 **Île aux Cerfs** – A scenic spot with **calm turquoise waters and beautiful beaches.**

🏄 **Grand Baie** – Ideal for **a leisurely paddle along the coastline.**

🏄 **Tamarin River** – A peaceful experience, paddling through **lush mangroves.**

Pro Tip: Try paddleboarding **at sunrise or sunset** for a magical experience on the water.

Deep-Sea Fishing: What to Expect and How to Book

Mauritius is a **world-class deep-sea fishing destination**, attracting anglers looking to catch **marlin, tuna, dorado,** and other trophy fish. The island's deep waters are home to some of the largest game fish, making it a **top destination for sport fishing.**

What to Expect on a Deep-Sea Fishing Trip

- **Target Species:** Blue marlin, black marlin, yellowfin tuna, dorado (mahi-mahi), wahoo, and sailfish.
- **Fishing Techniques:** Trolling, big-game fishing, and jigging.
- **Trip Duration:** Half-day (4-5 hours) or full-day (8+ hours) charters available.
- **Best Season:** October to April (peak marlin season), but great fishing is available year-round.

Best Deep-Sea Fishing Locations:

🎣 **Black River** – One of the **best starting points for deep-sea fishing**, with access to deep waters just minutes from shore.

🎣 **Grand Baie** – A popular spot for **half-day fishing charters**, targeting tuna and dorado.

🎣 **Le Morne** – Offers **deep waters close to shore**, ideal for marlin and wahoo fishing.

How to Book a Fishing Charter in Mauritius

When booking a fishing trip, look for:

■ **Reputable operators** with experienced captains.

■ **Modern, well-equipped boats** with fishing gear provided.

■ **Eco-conscious companies** that follow sustainable fishing practices.

Booking Tip: Reserve your trip in advance during peak fishing season, as slots fill up quickly. Most charters include **refreshments and expert guides**, ensuring an exciting and comfortable experience.

Golf Courses in Mauritius: Top Locations for Golf Enthusiasts

Mauritius is **one of the best golfing destinations in the Indian Ocean**, with **stunning courses designed by golf legends**. Whether you're a professional golfer or a casual player, the island offers **challenging layouts with breathtaking scenery**.

Top Golf Courses in Mauritius

⛳ **Île aux Cerfs Golf Club** – A spectacular **18-hole championship course** on a private island, designed by Bernhard Langer. **Accessible only by boat!**

⛳ **Heritage Golf Club (Bel Ombre)** – A **world-renowned course** featuring lush greens and ocean views.

⛳ **Mont Choisy Le Golf** – A **beautiful course in the north**, offering a mix of **open fairways and challenging bunkers**.

⛳ **Anahita Golf Club** – Designed by Ernie Els, this **par-72 course** sits along the stunning **east coast lagoons**.

⛳ **Avalon Golf Estate** – A unique inland course with **cooler temperatures and rolling green landscapes**.

🟦 **Best time to play golf in Mauritius:** May to October (cooler and drier weather).

Pro Tip: Many resorts offer **stay-and-play golf packages**, combining **luxury accommodations with unlimited golf rounds**.

Final Thoughts

Mauritius is a **dream destination** for travelers seeking adventure, excitement, and relaxation.

Whether you're **riding the waves on a kitesurf, reeling in a marlin on a deep-sea fishing trip, or teeing off on a world-class golf course**, the island has something for everyone.

With its **stunning scenery, warm waters, and top-tier facilities**, Mauritius ensures that every outdoor experience is **unforgettable**. So pack your gear, book your excursions, and get ready to **experience the thrill of Mauritius!**

CHAPTER ELEVEN
MAURITIUS' CULTURAL AND FESTIVE SCENE

Mauritius is a **vibrant melting pot of cultures, traditions, and celebrations,** shaped by its rich history and diverse population. With influences from **Indian, African, Chinese, and European heritage,** the island's **festivals, cultural centers, historic sites, and religious customs** offer travelers a **fascinating glimpse into its unique identity.**

Whether you're **attending a colorful festival, exploring a museum, or watching a live sega performance,** experiencing Mauritius' cultural scene is an essential part of any visit. This chapter provides a deep dive into the island's **most exciting events, must-visit cultural attractions, and important customs to respect.**

Local Festivals and Celebrations in 2025

Mauritius is known for its **spectacular festivals** that bring communities together in a vibrant display of **music, dance, food, and rituals.** Many of these celebrations are **rooted in religious traditions** but are widely enjoyed by both locals and visitors.

Major Festivals in Mauritius (2025 Calendar)

🎋 **Thaipusam Cavadee** (January 25, 2025)
A significant festival for the **Tamil community**, Thaipusam Cavadee is a deeply spiritual event marked by **prayers, fasting, and a grand procession**. Devotees carry **decorated wooden structures (cavadees)** and sometimes practice body piercing as a form of penance.

🏮 **Chinese New Year** (January 29, 2025) Celebrated by the island's **Chinese-Mauritian community**, the **Lunar New Year** is a time for **dragon dances, fireworks, and delicious feasts**. Chinatown in Port Louis is the best place to witness the festivities.

🕉 **Maha Shivaratri** (March 1, 2025) The largest Hindu festival in Mauritius, Maha Shivaratri, sees thousands of pilgrims walking to **Grand Bassin (Ganga Talao)**, a sacred lake. Devotees dress in white, chant prayers, and offer tributes to Lord Shiva.

🪔 **Holi – The Festival of Colors** (March 13, 2025)

Holi transforms Mauritius into a **colorful playground**, as people throw **vibrant powders, dance to Bollywood music, and share sweets**. It's one of the most joyful and inclusive celebrations on the island.

🕌 **Eid-ul-Fitr** (April 22, 2025 – Date Varies)
Marking the end of **Ramadan**, Eid-ul-Fitr is a major festival for the **Muslim community**. Families gather for **prayers, feasts, and acts of charity**, and visitors can sample special **Mauritian Muslim delicacies**.

🎭 **Sega Night and Creole Festival** (October 2025)
Dedicated to **Creole heritage**, this festival is a lively mix of **traditional Sega music, dance, and cuisine**. Expect energetic performances, storytelling, and a celebration of **Mauritian African roots**.

🪔 **Diwali – The Festival of Lights** (October 21, 2025)
One of the most dazzling celebrations in Mauritius, **Diwali** is marked by **glowing oil lamps, firework displays, and sweet treats**. Walking through **Triolet, Port Louis, and Quatre Bornes** during Diwali is a mesmerizing experience.

Cultural Centers and Live Performances

Mauritius is home to **various cultural institutions** that showcase **traditional music, dance, and performing arts**. Visiting these centers allows travelers to experience the island's **heritage firsthand**.

Top Cultural Centers & Performance Venues

🎭 **Caudan Arts Centre (Port Louis)** This modern venue hosts **theatre performances, music concerts, and art exhibitions**, making it the heart of the **contemporary arts scene** in Mauritius.

🥁 **Sega Music Performances** Sega is the **soul of Mauritian music**, originating from **African slave traditions**. To experience **authentic Sega**, visit:

- **Le Chamarel Restaurant** – Live Sega with traditional Creole dining.
- **Heritage Le Telfair** – A beachfront resort offering mesmerizing Sega shows.
- **La Rhumerie de Chamarel** – A rum distillery that frequently hosts Sega nights.

🏛 **Rajiv Gandhi Science Centre (Bell Village)**
A fascinating place to explore Mauritius' **scientific advancements and innovation**, featuring **interactive exhibits** for all ages.

🏮 **Chinese Cultural Centre (Port Louis)**
A great spot to learn about **Chinese-Mauritian traditions**, language, and calligraphy workshops.

🪔 **Indira Gandhi Centre for Indian Culture (Phoenix)**
This cultural hub promotes **Indian heritage**, hosting **Bharatanatyam dance shows, yoga sessions, and language classes.**

Historic Sites and Museums for Cultural Immersion

Mauritius has a **deep and complex history**, from **colonial influences** to **the legacy of indentured labor**. Exploring the island's museums and historic sites offers a **profound understanding of its past.**

Must-Visit Historic Sites and Museums

🏛 **Aapravasi Ghat (Port Louis)** – **UNESCO World Heritage Site** The **Aapravasi Ghat** is where **thousands of Indian indentured laborers** first arrived in Mauritius in the 19th century. This site tells the **emotional story of migration, struggle, and cultural transformation.**

🏛 **Eureka House (Moka)** A beautifully preserved **colonial-era mansion**, offering a glimpse into **Mauritius' 19th-century plantation lifestyle.**

⚓ **Blue Penny Museum (Port Louis)** Famous for housing the **rare 1847 "Blue Penny" and "Red Penny" stamps**, this museum is perfect for **history and philately enthusiasts.**

🪴 **Château de Labourdonnais (Mapou)** This **stunning 19th-century estate** showcases **Mauritian aristocracy, Creole architecture, and lush gardens.**

🪴 **Le Morne Cultural Landscape – UNESCO World Heritage Site** Le Morne is a **symbol of resistance** and a memorial to **enslaved people who sought refuge on the mountain.** The surrounding area is also breathtakingly beautiful.

Religious and Traditional Practices to Respect

Mauritius is a **multi-religious country** where **Hinduism, Islam, Christianity, and Buddhism coexist harmoniously.** While visitors are welcome to observe religious practices, **respecting local customs is essential.**

Etiquette When Visiting Temples, Mosques, and Churches

🕉 **Dress Modestly** – Cover shoulders and knees when entering **Hindu temples, mosques, and churches.**

🕉 **Remove Shoes** – Always take off your shoes before entering **religious sites.**

🕉 **Avoid Public Displays of Affection** – In sacred spaces, be mindful of cultural sensitivity.

🕉 **Photography Rules** – Always ask before taking pictures inside temples or mosques.

Traditional Customs to Observe

- **Offering a "Namaste" or "Bonjour"** – A respectful way to greet locals.

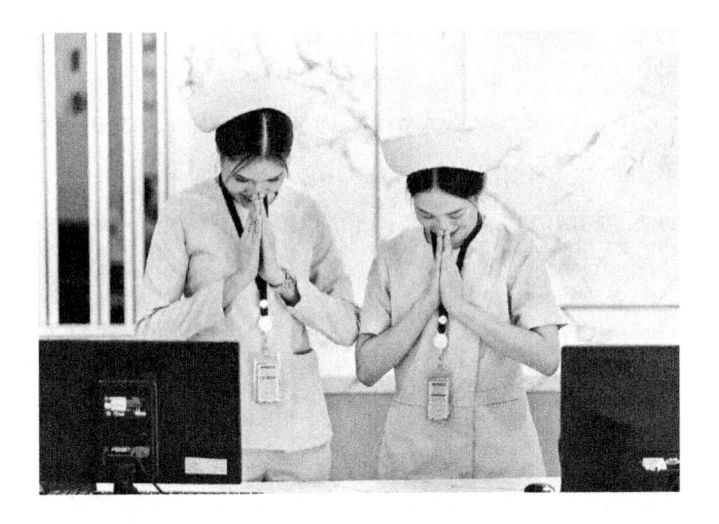

- **Gifting Sweets During Diwali or Eid** – If invited to a local home, bringing sweets is a thoughtful gesture.

- **Respecting Elders** – Showing courtesy and addressing elders with respect is an important cultural norm.

Final Thoughts

Mauritius is more than just a tropical paradise—it is **a land of traditions, celebrations, and cultural richness.**

From **lively festivals and heritage sites to mesmerizing Sega music and sacred temples**, every aspect of Mauritian culture tells a story of **resilience, diversity, and unity.**

By immersing yourself in the **island's cultural and festive scene**, you'll gain a **deeper appreciation for the people and their way of life**. So, whether you're **dancing under the stars at a Sega night or exploring a colonial mansion**, embrace every moment and **let Mauritius captivate your heart.**

CHAPTER ELEVEN
HEALTH, SAFETY, AND PRACTICAL INFORMATION

When planning a trip to **Mauritius in 2025**, it's important to be well-prepared in terms of **health, safety, and accessibility**. While Mauritius is one of the **safest travel destinations in the Indian Ocean**, taking necessary precautions can ensure a **stress-free and enjoyable experience**.

This chapter provides **essential health guidelines, safety tips, emergency contacts, and advice for travelers with disabilities**, helping you navigate the island with confidence.

Vaccinations and Health Precautions

Mauritius has **a high standard of healthcare**, but travelers should take **certain health precautions** to stay well during their visit.

Recommended Vaccinations for Mauritius (2025 Update)

While no vaccinations are **mandatory** for entry, the following are **recommended**:

✈ **Routine Vaccines** – Ensure you are up to date on standard vaccinations such as **MMR (measles, mumps, rubella), diphtheria-tetanus-pertussis (DTP), and polio**.

🦠 **Hepatitis A & B** – Mauritius' food hygiene standards are high, but **Hepatitis A** can still be contracted through contaminated food or water. **Hepatitis B** is recommended for those engaging in **medical procedures or close contact sports**.

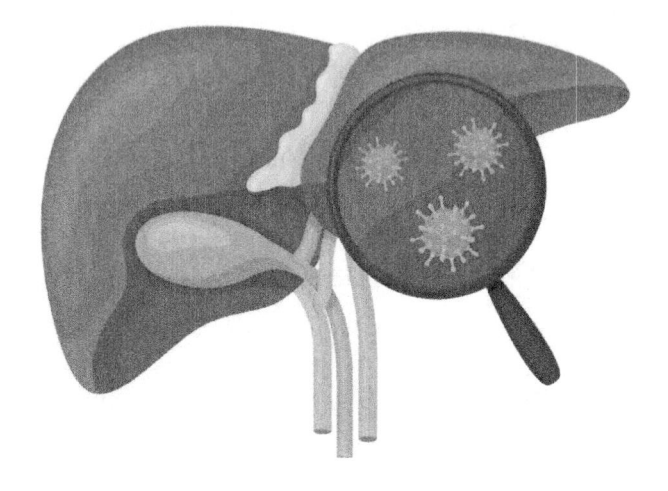

● **Typhoid** – This vaccine is suggested for travelers planning to explore **rural areas or trying street food extensively**.

🦟 **Dengue Fever Prevention** – Dengue is **present in Mauritius**, and while no vaccine exists, **mosquito bite prevention** is essential. Use **DEET-based insect repellents**, wear **long sleeves**, and stay in accommodations with **mosquito nets or air conditioning**.

- **Rabies (For Adventure Travelers)** – Though rare, rabies exists in **bats and stray animals**. Consider this vaccine if hiking, camping, or working with animals.

- **Malaria** – Mauritius has been **malaria-free since 1997**, so **antimalarial medication is not required**.

Food and Water Safety

- **Tap water** in major towns and hotels is **generally safe**, but it's advisable to drink **bottled or filtered water**.

- Eat at **reputable restaurants** and be cautious with **street food** to avoid foodborne illnesses.

- Avoid consuming **raw seafood or undercooked meats** in remote areas.

Sun Protection and Heat Precautions

Mauritius' **tropical climate** means high temperatures and strong UV rays. Protect yourself by:

☀ **Using SPF 50+ sunscreen** (reef-safe preferred)

💧 **Staying hydrated** with at least 2 liters of water daily

🧢 **Wearing a hat and sunglasses**

🕶 **Seeking shade between 11 AM and 3 PM**

Safety Tips for Travelers: Crime, Weather, and Emergencies

Mauritius is **one of the safest destinations** in the world, but travelers should always **exercise caution.**

Crime and Personal Safety

🎒 **Petty Theft:** While violent crime is **rare**, petty theft such as **pickpocketing and bag snatching** can occur in busy markets and beaches.

● **Avoid Flashy Displays:** Keep **expensive jewelry and electronics** discreet, especially in **Port Louis and Grand Baie.**

🌙 **Night Safety:** Stick to **well-lit, populated areas at night**, and avoid **walking alone on deserted beaches.**

■ **Secure Your Belongings:** Use hotel **safes for passports, cash, and valuables**, and withdraw money only from **trusted ATMs** inside banks.

Weather and Natural Hazards

Mauritius experiences **two main seasons**:

🌴 **Summer (November–April):** Warm and humid with occasional **cyclones (January–March)**. Keep an eye on **local weather updates** and follow hotel or government advisories.

❄ Winter (May–October): Mild and dry, perfect for **outdoor activities**. The ocean may be **rougher on the east coast**, making some water sports **more challenging**.

Swimming and Water Safety

🌊 **Strong Currents:** Some beaches, especially on the **southern and eastern coasts**, have **strong tides and rip currents**. Always swim in **designated safe areas**.

🚩 **Check Warning Flags:** Red flags indicate **unsafe conditions**; follow lifeguard instructions.

🐚 **Marine Hazards:** Be cautious of **sea urchins, jellyfish, and coral cuts** when snorkeling. Wearing **reef-safe footwear** is advised.

Road Safety

🚗 **Drive on the Left:** Mauritius follows the **British driving system**, so vehicles drive on the **left-hand side**.

🚦 **Traffic Conditions:** Roads are generally well-maintained, but expect **narrow streets and aggressive drivers** in cities.

🛵 **Scooter Rentals:** If renting a **motorbike or scooter**, always **wear a helmet** and avoid **driving at night** in rural areas.

Local Emergency Numbers and Services

In case of an emergency, knowing the **right contacts** can be a lifesaver.

📞 **Emergency Hotlines in Mauritius (2025 Update)**

🚔 **Police:** 999 or 112
🚑 **Ambulance:** 114
🔥 **Fire and Rescue:** 115
⚓ **Coast Guard:** 177

Hospitals and Medical Facilities

Mauritius has **high-quality private hospitals** and **public healthcare facilities**. For non-emergencies, visiting a private clinic ensures **faster service**.

🏥 **Recommended Hospitals for Tourists**

✔️ **Wellkin Hospital (Moka)** – Top private hospital with **English-speaking doctors**.

✔️ **Clinique Darné (Floreal)** – Excellent for **urgent care and specialist consultations**.

✔️ **City Clinic (Grand Baie)** – Convenient for **northern coast travelers**.

🟢 **Pharmacies (Chemists)** – Easily found across the island, usually marked by a **green cross**. Most open **8 AM – 8 PM**, with some **24-hour options in cities**.

Accessible Travel: Tips for Travelers with Disabilities

Mauritius is gradually improving its **accessibility**, but challenges remain. Here's what travelers with **mobility impairments, visual disabilities, or special needs** should know.

Airport and Transport Accessibility

✈ Sir Seewoosagur Ramgoolam International Airport (SSR) is **wheelchair-friendly**, with:

- Elevators and accessible restrooms
- Assistance services (pre-booking required)
- Priority boarding

- **Taxis and Private Transfers:** Some companies offer **wheelchair-friendly vehicles** (book in advance).

- **Public Transport:** Buses are **not wheelchair-accessible**, so private transport is **recommended**.

Accessible Hotels and Resorts

Several high-end hotels in Mauritius offer **fully accessible rooms** with ramps, roll-in showers, and elevators. Recommended options include:

- **Shangri-La Le Touessrok** – Spacious, step-free rooms and accessible restaurants.

- *LUX Belle Mare** – Wheelchair-friendly suites and adapted beach access.

- **Four Seasons Resort Mauritius** – Personalized assistance and adapted excursions.

Beaches and Attractions with Accessibility

- **Mont Choisy Beach** – Offers **smooth walkways** and **adapted facilities**.

- **Sir Seewoosagur Ramgoolam Botanical Garden** – Wheelchair-friendly paths for **scenic exploration**.

🏛 **Grand Bassin Temple** – Some areas have **ramps for visitors with limited mobility**.

Final Thoughts

With the **right precautions**, Mauritius is a **safe, healthy, and enjoyable** destination for all travelers. Whether you're planning an **adventure-filled trip, a relaxing getaway, or an accessible holiday**, being prepared with **health and safety knowledge** will help you make the most of your time on this stunning island.

By following these guidelines, you'll **stay safe, healthy, and ready** to explore everything Mauritius has to offer in 2025!

CHAPTER TWELVE
DAY TRIPS AND EXCURSIONS

Mauritius is a paradise in itself, but beyond its stunning beaches and lush landscapes lie **incredible day-trip destinations** that add even more depth to your journey. From **island-hopping adventures and marine wildlife encounters** to **historical plantations and cultural experiences**, Mauritius offers **a diverse range of excursions** that cater to every traveler's interest.

In this chapter, we explore some of the **most rewarding day trips** in Mauritius, including the remote **Rodrigues Island**, the iconic **Île aux Cerfs**, thrilling **dolphin and whale-watching tours**, and immersive **plantation visits** that highlight Mauritius' rich agricultural history.

Visiting Rodrigues Island: What to See and Do

Rodrigues Island is **a hidden gem** that sits about **560 kilometers (350 miles) east of Mauritius** in the Indian Ocean. This small volcanic island, just **18 kilometers long and 8 kilometers wide**, is often called **the "Mauritian Outback"** due to its **rugged beauty, slower pace of life, and untouched nature**. Unlike the bustling beaches of Mauritius, Rodrigues offers a **quieter, more traditional island experience**, making it **perfect for a one- or two-day trip.**

How to Get to Rodrigues

✈ **By Air** – Air Mauritius operates **daily flights** from Mauritius to Rodrigues, taking **about 90 minutes**.

⚓ **By Sea** – Cargo and passenger ships make the journey, but the trip takes **around 36 hours**, making flying the **best option for a day trip**.

Top Attractions on Rodrigues Island

🏛 **Port Mathurin** – The capital of Rodrigues, where you can **stroll through vibrant markets, meet friendly locals, and taste authentic Creole cuisine**.

🏖 **Trou d'Argent Beach** – A secluded paradise surrounded by cliffs, accessible via a **scenic hike through the Rodrigues countryside**.

🐦 **Ile aux Cocos** – A tiny **bird sanctuary island** where thousands of **white terns** and **noddies** nest. The crystal-clear waters surrounding the island are **ideal for snorkeling**.

🐙 **Octopus Fishing with Locals** – Experience **traditional fishing methods** with the island's fishermen, a unique way to learn about Rodrigues' **sustainable seafood culture**.

🧘 **Caverne Patate** – A **massive underground cave system** with dramatic rock formations, perfect for a short spelunking adventure.

Rodrigues offers a **refreshing change of pace** from the main island, making it **a must-visit for travelers looking for authenticity and raw natural beauty**.

Île aux Cerfs and Other Nearby Islands

A trip to Mauritius is incomplete without **exploring its stunning offshore islands**, and **Île aux Cerfs** is the most famous of them all.

Île aux Cerfs: The Ultimate Island Escape

Île aux Cerfs, or **"Deer Island,"** is a **tropical paradise** located off the east coast of Mauritius, near **Trou d'Eau Douce**. Though it no longer has deer, it boasts **some of the most breathtaking white-sand beaches and turquoise lagoons** in the region.

Getting to Île aux Cerfs

🛥 **By Speedboat or Catamaran** – Daily tours leave from **Trou d'Eau Douce** and take about **20 minutes**.

🛶 **By Kayak** – For adventure lovers, kayaking from the east coast is an option, taking about **1.5 hours**.

Things to Do on Île aux Cerfs

Relax on Stunning Beaches – The island's **pristine shores and shallow waters** make it ideal for **swimming and sunbathing**.

Play Golf on an Island Course – The Île aux Cerfs Golf Club, designed by Bernhard Langer, offers an **unforgettable golfing experience surrounded by ocean views**.

Try Water Sports – Enjoy activities like **parasailing, jet skiing, and snorkeling** in the island's warm, clear waters.

Dine in a Beachfront Restaurant – Savor **fresh seafood and Mauritian delicacies** at one of the island's **exclusive beach bars and restaurants**.

Other Nearby Islands Worth Exploring

Île aux Aigrettes – A **nature reserve dedicated to the conservation of endemic species** like the **Mauritian kestrel and giant tortoise**.

Île aux Benitiers – Famous for **Crystal Rock**, a natural coral formation rising out of the sea, and a **popular stop for dolphin-watching tours**.

Île aux Serpents – A **wild, uninhabited island** home to rare **booby birds** and breathtaking coastal views.

Each island has **its unique charm**, making island-hopping one of the **most rewarding experiences in Mauritius**.

Dolphin and Whale Watching Tours

Mauritius is one of the **best places in the world to see dolphins and whales in their natural habitat**. The island's **warm, clear waters** provide a perfect environment for **marine wildlife**, and several **eco-friendly tour operators** offer responsible encounters.

Dolphin Watching in Mauritius

🐬 **Best Spots:** The most famous area for dolphin-watching is **Tamarin Bay**, located on the west coast. Here, you'll see **pods of spinner and bottlenose dolphins** playing in the morning sun.

⏰ **Best Time to Go:** Dolphins are most active **early in the morning (6 AM - 9 AM)**.

🐋 Swim with Dolphins (Ethically) – Some tours offer the chance to **swim with wild dolphins**, but always choose an **eco-conscious operator** that follows **strict guidelines** to avoid stressing the animals.

Whale Watching in Mauritius

Mauritius is home to **two types of whales**:

🐋 **Sperm Whales** – Found **year-round**, especially in **deep waters off the west coast**.

🐋 **Humpback Whales** – Seen **between June and October**, when they migrate through Mauritian waters.

➤ **Best Tours:** The best whale-watching tours depart from **Black River**, using hydrophones to locate these magnificent creatures.

Seeing these **gentle giants** in the wild is **an unforgettable experience**, making this excursion a highlight of any trip to Mauritius.

Plantation Tours: Sugarcane and Tea Estates

Mauritius has a **rich agricultural history**, and a visit to one of its **historic plantations** offers a fascinating glimpse into the island's **colonial past, economic evolution, and culinary culture**.

Sugarcane Plantations

Sugar production has shaped **Mauritius' economy** for centuries. Today, some of the island's **best sugarcane estates** welcome visitors to learn about **the production process and the history of slavery and indentured labor**.

🏛 **L'Aventure du Sucre (The Sugar Adventure)** – Located in **Pamplemousses**, this museum tells the story of **sugar's role in Mauritius' history**. Guests can also **sample over 15 types of raw and refined sugars**.

🌿 **Saint Aubin Sugar Estate** – One of the oldest plantations in Mauritius, offering **rum tastings, vanilla plantations, and a Creole lunch experience**.

Tea Plantations

Mauritius is also known for its **unique tea culture**, influenced by British traditions and local flavors.

🍇 **Bois Chéri Tea Plantation** – The largest tea estate in Mauritius, offering **scenic tours of tea fields, a factory visit, and a tea-tasting session** overlooking the countryside.

🍇 **Domaine des Aubineaux** – A colonial mansion surrounded by **lush tea fields**, where visitors can learn about **traditional tea production**.

Visiting a **plantation** is not just about learning—it's about **tasting the rich flavors of Mauritius** and experiencing the **deep cultural ties** these crops have to the island's identity.

Final Thoughts

From **untouched islands and marine encounters** to **historical estates and cultural gems**, Mauritius offers **unforgettable excursions** that showcase the island's **natural** beauty and heritage. Whether you're an **adventure seeker, history buff, or wildlife lover,** these day trips will add a **new dimension to your journey** and make your **Mauritius 2025 experience truly extraordinary!**

CHAPTER THIRTEEN
SAMPLE ITINERARIES

Planning a trip to **Mauritius** can be exciting, but with so much to see and do, it's easy to feel overwhelmed. Whether you're visiting for a **short getaway, a week-long vacation, or an extended stay**, having a well-structured **itinerary** can help you make the most of your time.

This chapter provides **detailed day-by-day itineraries** tailored for different types of travelers. Whether you're seeking **relaxation, adventure, cultural experiences, or a mix of everything**, these plans ensure you experience the best of Mauritius without feeling rushed.

3-Day Itinerary for a Quick Getaway

A short trip to Mauritius means focusing on the **absolute must-see attractions** while leaving room for relaxation. This itinerary is **ideal for weekend travelers, business visitors with limited free time, or those combining Mauritius with another destination**.

Day 1: Arrival and Beach Relaxation

✈ **Morning:** Arrive at **Sir Seewoosagur Ramgoolam International Airport (MRU)** and check into a beachfront resort in the **Grand Baie or Flic en Flac area**.

🏖 Afternoon: Unwind at the **stunning beaches** of Flic en Flac or Trou aux Biches. Enjoy **swimming, sunbathing, or snorkeling in crystal-clear waters.**

🍷 Evening: Head to **Grand Baie** for a **seafront dinner** at a local seafood restaurant and experience the island's **vibrant nightlife.**

Day 2: South Mauritius Exploration

⛰ Morning: Visit **Chamarel Seven Colored Earth** and witness **the surreal rainbow-hued sand dunes.** Stop by **Chamarel Waterfall,** the **tallest waterfall in Mauritius.**

🍂 Afternoon: Explore **Black River Gorges National Park** for a light hike and a chance to spot **rare wildlife like the Mauritius kestrel.**

🌑 Evening: Dine at **Le Chamarel Restaurant,** where you can enjoy **panoramic sunset views** and delicious **Creole cuisine.**

Day 3: Island Adventure

🚤 Morning: Take a **speedboat tour** to **Île aux Cerfs,** a **tropical paradise** known for **white sandy beaches, snorkeling spots, and water sports.**

🍖 Afternoon: Have a **beachside BBQ lunch** on the island and soak in the tranquil lagoon.

- **Evening:** Return to the main island, explore **Caudan Waterfront for last-minute shopping**, and head to the airport for departure.

7-Day Itinerary for First-Time Visitors

A week in Mauritius allows you to experience **the island's diverse landscapes, rich culture, and unique wildlife**, balancing **adventure, history, and relaxation**.

Day 1: Arrival and Beach Time

- Arrive in **Mauritius and check in to a beachfront hotel**.
- Spend the afternoon at **Mont Choisy Beach**, one of the island's most picturesque shores.
- Enjoy a sunset dinner at **La Plage Beach Club**.

Day 2: Northern Mauritius – Port Louis & Grand Baie

- Visit **Port Louis' Central Market** for local crafts and street food.
- Explore **Aapravasi Ghat**, a UNESCO site showcasing Mauritius' indentured labor history.
- Enjoy water sports or relax at **Grand Baie Beach**.

Day 3: East Coast & Île aux Cerfs

- Take a **catamaran cruise** to **Île aux Cerfs** for **snorkeling and parasailing.**
- Explore the **Grande Rivière Sud Est Waterfall** by boat.
- Return to your resort for a leisurely evening.

Day 4: Wildlife & Nature

- Visit **Casela Nature Parks** for a **quad biking safari** among zebras and giraffes.
- Explore **Ebony Forest Reserve** for a guided trek through **restored native forests.**

Day 5: Chamarel & Black River Gorges

- Discover **Chamarel Seven Colored Earth** and **Chamarel Waterfall.**
- Hike in **Black River Gorges National Park.**
- Visit a **local rum distillery** for a tasting experience.

Day 6: West Coast & Dolphin Watching

- Take a **morning boat trip from Tamarin Bay** to see **wild dolphins.**

- Explore **Le Morne Brabant**, a UNESCO-listed mountain with breathtaking views.
- Enjoy a **Creole dinner** at a local restaurant.

Day 7: Relaxation & Departure

- Spend your last day at **Flic en Flac Beach** or pamper yourself with a **luxury spa treatment**.
- Depart for the airport with unforgettable memories.

10-Day Itinerary for a Well-Rounded Experience

A **10-day trip** allows you to explore **both popular and off-the-beaten-path destinations**, fully immersing yourself in Mauritius' landscapes, history, and vibrant local life.

Days 1-3: Port Louis, Grand Baie & Northern Attractions

- Explore **Caudan Waterfront, Central Market, and Chinatown** in Port Louis.
- Visit **SSR Botanical Garden** in Pamplemousses.
- Enjoy **a luxury catamaran cruise** along the northern coast.

Days 4-5: East Coast & Rodrigues Island

- Take a **day trip to Île aux Cerfs** for snorkeling and water sports.

- Fly to **Rodrigues Island** for a **two-day off-the-grid adventure** featuring **hiking, caves, and fishing villages.**

Days 6-7: South Mauritius & Le Morne

- Visit **Bois Chéri Tea Plantation** for a guided tour and tasting.

- Hike **Le Morne Brabant**, a mountain with a tragic yet powerful history.

- Discover the **wild beaches of Gris Gris**, where powerful waves crash against dramatic cliffs.

Days 8-9: Dolphin Watching, Chamarel & Black River Gorges

- Go **dolphin-watching in Tamarin Bay** and snorkel in Blue Bay Marine Park.
- Visit **Chamarel's Seven Colored Earth, Black River Gorges, and a local rum distillery**.

Day 10: Beach & Departure

- Spend your last day at **La Cuvette Beach** or pamper yourself with a **luxury spa treatment** before heading home.

Customizable Itinerary Suggestions for Different Travelers

Depending on your interests, you might want to **tailor your trip** to focus on a particular theme. Here are some **customized itinerary ideas**:

For Adventure Seekers

- Quad biking in **Casela Nature Parks**
- Hiking **Le Morne Brabant**
- Diving at **Blue Bay Marine Park**
- Windsurfing at **Belle Mare**

For Couples & Honeymooners

- Private **catamaran cruise to Île aux Cerfs**
- Sunset **dinner at Le Château de Bel Ombre**
- Spa retreat at a **luxury resort**
- Romantic **picnic at Trou d'Argent Beach (Rodrigues Island)**

For Families with Kids

- Visit **La Vanille Nature Park** to see giant tortoises and crocodiles.
- Enjoy **Casela's interactive animal encounters.**
- Try **glass-bottom boat rides and snorkeling** at Blue Bay.
- Explore **Curious Corner of Chamarel**, a fun, interactive museum.

For Culture & History Enthusiasts

- Walk through **Port Louis' colonial sites.**
- Learn about **indentured labor history at Aapravasi Ghat.**
- Visit **Eureka House**, an old Creole mansion.

- Explore **traditional fishing villages like Mahébourg**.

Final Thoughts

Mauritius is an island of **endless discovery**, and whether you're visiting for **three days or two weeks**, there's always something new to experience. These **carefully crafted itineraries** ensure you **maximize your time**, whether you prefer **relaxation, adventure, or cultural immersion**.

No matter what kind of traveler you are, Mauritius promises an **unforgettable journey** filled with **pristine beaches, lush landscapes, thrilling excursions, and rich history.**

CHAPTER FOURTEEN
SUSTAINABILITY AND RESPONSIBLE TOURISM IN MAURITIUS

Mauritius is often described as a **paradise island**, renowned for its **pristine beaches, lush forests, and vibrant marine life**. However, with increasing tourism, it has become more important than ever to embrace **sustainable and responsible travel** practices to protect this **delicate ecosystem** and ensure that local communities benefit from tourism.

As a visitor, you have the power to make a **positive impact** by choosing **eco-conscious accommodations, supporting conservation efforts, engaging with local businesses, and respecting the island's cultural and environmental heritage**. This chapter provides practical insights on how to experience Mauritius **ethically and sustainably**, while still enjoying everything this tropical destination has to offer.

Eco-Friendly Accommodations and Tours

One of the most effective ways to support sustainability in Mauritius is by **choosing accommodations and tour operators** that prioritize **environmental conservation, energy efficiency, and community involvement.**

Several hotels, lodges, and tourism services have taken proactive steps to minimize their carbon footprint while offering guests **an unforgettable experience in harmony with nature.**

Green Hotels and Resorts

When selecting where to stay, look for properties that have received certifications such as:

■ **Green Key Certification** – Recognizes hotels that meet strict sustainability criteria.

■ **EarthCheck Certification** – Focuses on **eco-friendly operations and waste reduction.**

■ **Mauritian Eco-Label** – A local certification highlighting responsible tourism initiatives.

Some **noteworthy eco-conscious accommodations** in Mauritius include:

🌴 **Lakaz Chamarel Exclusive Lodge** – Nestled in **Chamarel's lush hills**, this boutique lodge emphasizes **rainwater harvesting, solar energy, and organic gardening.**

🌱 **Salt of Palmar** – A sustainable beachfront hotel that operates **plastic-free, sources ingredients from local farmers, and supports community projects.**

- Bubble Lodge at Île aux Cerfs – An eco-luxury retreat with minimal impact on the island's environment.

Responsible Tour Operators

Eco-friendly tour operators play a crucial role in **minimizing harm to Mauritius' ecosystems** while providing immersive experiences. Look for tours that:

- Use **electric or low-emission boats** for marine excursions.
- Avoid **feeding wildlife or disturbing natural habitats**.
- Work with **local guides and conservation organizations**.

Some recommended operators include:

Mauritian Wildlife Foundation Tours – Focuses on **educational eco-tours** to protected areas.

Dolswim Dolphin Tours – Offers **ethical dolphin-watching experiences** without chasing or disturbing marine life.

🌿 **Otentic Eco Tents** – Provides a **sustainable adventure experience in Mauritius' forests and rivers.**

Volunteering Opportunities and Community-Based Tourism

For travelers looking to **give back**, Mauritius offers numerous opportunities to **engage with local communities, support conservation projects, and promote sustainable development.** Volunteering allows visitors to **gain deeper insights into the island's culture, biodiversity, and environmental challenges** while making a meaningful contribution.

Volunteering with Conservation Projects

If you're passionate about **wildlife protection, reforestation, or marine conservation**, consider joining projects such as:

🌿 **Mauritian Wildlife Foundation (MWF)** – Supports **native species conservation and habitat restoration.**

🪸 **Blue Lagoon Marine Conservation** – Works on **coral reef restoration and marine biodiversity preservation.**

🌳 **Ebony Forest Reserve** – Allows volunteers to **participate in reforestation and guided ecological education programs.**

Community-Based Tourism (CBT)

Engaging in **community-based tourism** allows travelers to experience **authentic Mauritian culture while directly supporting local livelihoods**. Some enriching CBT activities include:

🏡 **Staying in a Mauritian homestay** – Experience **traditional island life** with a local family.

🎨 **Learning local crafts** – Join workshops on **traditional basket weaving, pottery, and wood carving.**

🍲 **Cooking with locals** – Take a **Creole cooking class** and learn to prepare dishes like **Dholl Puri and Rougaille.**

By participating in these initiatives, visitors **not only enrich their travel experience but also contribute to the empowerment of local communities.**

Wildlife Conservation Tips and Practices

Mauritius is home to a variety of **unique flora and fauna**, including **rare birds, endemic reptiles, and fragile marine ecosystems.** Unfortunately, habitat destruction, pollution, and climate change pose **significant threats** to these species. As a responsible traveler, you can help protect Mauritius' wildlife by following **ethical tourism practices.**

Respecting Marine Life

🐚 **Avoid touching or stepping on coral reefs** – Corals are **delicate living organisms** that take decades to grow but can be destroyed in seconds.

🐟 **Do not feed fish or marine animals** – This disrupts their **natural behaviors** and can cause long-term harm.

🐬 **Choose ethical marine tours** – Avoid operators that chase dolphins or allow direct interaction with wild sea creatures.

Protecting Land Wildlife

- **Support wildlife sanctuaries, not petting zoos** – Ethical sanctuaries focus on **rehabilitation and conservation**, while petting zoos often exploit animals.

- **Stick to marked trails when hiking** – This prevents damage to **fragile ecosystems**.

- **Do not purchase souvenirs made from endangered species** – Items made from **turtle shells, coral, or rare wood** contribute to illegal wildlife trade.

By adopting these small but significant habits, you play an essential role in **preserving Mauritius' extraordinary biodiversity**.

Supporting Local Businesses and Artisans

Tourism plays a vital role in Mauritius' economy, but large-scale commercial enterprises often **overshadow small businesses and local artisans**. To ensure your spending benefits the **local population**, consider **shopping, dining, and engaging with businesses that prioritize sustainability and cultural preservation**.

Buy Authentic, Locally-Made Souvenirs

Instead of mass-produced goods, opt for:

- 🪢 **Handmade Mauritian crafts** – Such as **woven baskets, wood carvings, and hand-dyed textiles.**

- 🍯 **Locally-produced food products** – Such as **Mauritian vanilla, artisanal honey, and sugarcane rum.**

- 👗 **Ethical fashion** – Brands like EcoMauritius.mu promote sustainable clothing made from organic materials.

Eat at Locally-Owned Restaurants

Instead of dining at large international chains, **support small Creole eateries and family-run restaurants.** This ensures **authentic food experiences** while contributing directly to **local livelihoods.** Some great choices include:

- 🍲 **Escale Créole** – A **hidden gem for traditional Mauritian dishes.**

- 🐟 **Le Off in Grand Baie** – Serves **freshly caught seafood from local fishermen.**

🌿 **La Maison Eureka** – A historic plantation house serving farm-to-table meals.

Use Local Tour Guides

Hiring **licensed Mauritian guides** ensures that **tourism revenue stays within the community,** while also providing a more authentic and educational experience.

Final Thoughts

Sustainable tourism is **not about sacrificing comfort or experiences**—it's about **traveling in a way that respects and preserves the beauty of Mauritius** for future generations. By making **small but conscious choices,** such as **staying in eco-friendly lodges, supporting local artisans, and** respecting wildlife, you contribute to a **greener, more responsible tourism industry.**

Mauritius is more than just a **holiday destination**—it is a **living, breathing ecosystem with a rich cultural heritage.** When you travel with awareness, you **not only enjoy its wonders but also ensure they remain for generations to come.**

CHAPTER FIFTEEN

USEFUL CONTACTS AND RESOURCES FOR TRAVELERS IN MAURITIUS

When traveling to a new destination, having quick access to essential contacts and resources is crucial for a **smooth and safe experience**. Mauritius, known for its **idyllic landscapes** and **friendly locals**, is no different. Whether you need **tourist information, medical assistance, or embassy support**, knowing where to turn can make all the difference. This chapter provides vital contact details and resources to help you **navigate Mauritius with confidence** in 2025.

Tourist Information Centers

Mauritius is well-equipped with **tourist information centers** strategically located across the island, offering **helpful resources, guides,** and **maps** to ensure visitors have a seamless stay. These centers are **knowledgeable** and provide insights on **local attractions, transportation,** and **cultural norms**, as well as **up-to-date event listings** and **practical travel tips**.

Here are some key tourist information centers in Mauritius:

1. Mauritius Tourism Authority (MTA)

Location:

📍 Tourism House, Caudan Waterfront, Port Louis

The **Mauritius Tourism Authority (MTA)** is the national body for tourism-related information. They provide **brochures, guides,** and **personalized assistance** to tourists. Whether you're looking for suggestions on **local activities**, need directions, or are in search of **cultural experiences**, MTA staff are always ready to help.

Contact Info:

📞 +230 213 7800

✉ info@mauritius-tourism.mu

🌐 www.tourism-mauritius.mu

2. The InterContinental Resort Mauritius Information Desk

Location:

📍 Balaclava, North-West Mauritius

Situated inside one of the island's premium resorts, this information desk provides **guides** for **north coast activities**, local **adventure tours**, and **leisure experiences** in Mauritius.

Contact Info:

📞 +230 405 8888

✉ resort@intercontinental.com

3. Flic en Flac Tourist Office

Location:

📍 Flic en Flac, West Coast

For those staying on the **west coast** of Mauritius, the **Flic en Flac Tourist Office** is an ideal spot for **beach enthusiasts** seeking **water sports activities, local restaurants,** and **excursion details.** The staff are friendly and always offer detailed **local insight** into nearby attractions.

Contact Info:

📞 +230 453 3838

✉ info@flicenflac.mu

Emergency Numbers and Medical Facilities

While Mauritius is generally a safe destination for tourists, it's always best to be prepared for unexpected situations. The island has an efficient **emergency response system**, and there are plenty of **medical facilities** that cater to both tourists and locals. In case of emergencies, it's crucial to have **immediate access to local medical services** and **emergency contact numbers.**

Emergency Numbers

For a wide range of emergencies, the following numbers should be kept handy:

- Police: 📞 999 or 112
- Ambulance: 📞 114
- Fire Services: 📞 115
- Rescue Services (Coast Guard): 📞 999
- Tourist Assistance Service: 📞 +230 213 7800

Medical Facilities

Mauritius has several **private and public hospitals**, with excellent standards of care for both **routine treatments** and **emergency cases**. Below are a few well-regarded medical centers and their contact details:

1. Wellkin Hospital

Location:

📍 Beau Bassin, Port Louis

Wellkin Hospital offers **24/7 emergency services** and **specialist care** across various disciplines, from **cardiology** to **pediatrics**. It's one of the most popular private hospitals in

Mauritius and caters to international travelers with English-speaking staff.

Contact Info:

📞 +230 464 0300

✉ info@wellkinhospital.com

2. SSRN Hospital (Dr. A. G. Jeetoo Hospital)

Location:

📍 Port Louis

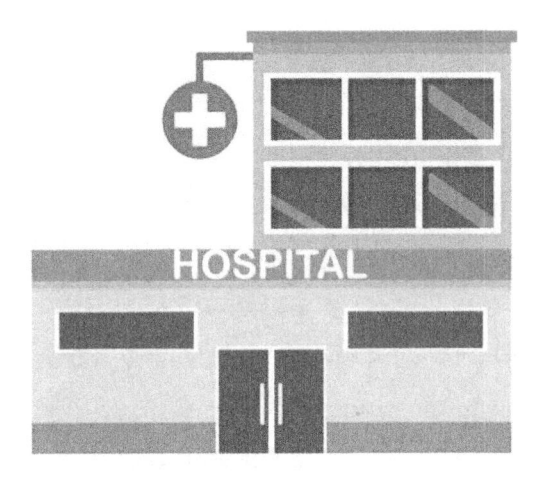

As the **largest public hospital** in Mauritius, **SSRN Hospital** offers **comprehensive medical services**, including **trauma care** and **infectious disease treatment**. It's an important facility for serious emergencies but can also cater to **less urgent needs**.

Contact Info:

📞 +230 203 2299

✉ ssrn@health.gov.mu

3. Mediclinic

Location:

📍 Grand Baie, North Coast

A premium medical facility with **English-speaking doctors, private rooms**, and **specialized care**. Mediclinic is ideal for travelers needing **medical check-ups** or **treatments in a private setting**.

Contact Info:

📞 +230 263 2899

✉ info@mediclinic.mu

Embassy and Consulate Contact Information

If you find yourself in a situation where you need **assistance from your home country** while in Mauritius, knowing the location and contact details of your **embassy or consulate** is crucial. Whether it's a **lost passport**, **legal matters**, or general consular services, your embassy is there to offer assistance.

1. The British High Commission

Location:

📍 12, Les Rivières Noires, Port Louis

The British High Commission is responsible for consular services for **UK citizens**, including **passport services, visas,** and **emergency assistance.**

Contact Info:

📞 +230 202 1300

✉ BritishHighCommission@fco.gov.uk

🌐 www.gov.uk/world/organisations/british-high-commission-port-louis

2. The United States Embassy

Location:

📍 Cnr. John Kennedy St., Port Louis

The U.S. Embassy provides consular support to **American citizens** in Mauritius, including **visa applications**, **emergency repatriation**, and **general support**.

Contact Info:

📞 +230 202 4400

✉ ConsularPortLouis@state.gov

🌐 mu.usembassy.gov

3. The French Embassy

Location:

📍 21, Avenue Pasteur, Port Louis

The French Embassy is a **vital resource** for **French nationals** and provides consular services such as **passports, birth registrations**, and emergency help for its citizens.

Contact Info:

📞 +230 202 4444

✉ ambassade.france@diplomatie.gouv.fr

🌐 maurice.ambafrance.org

4. The Indian High Commission

Location:

📍 Port Louis, Mauritius

The **Indian High Commission** offers consular assistance to **Indian nationals**, including **passport services, visa applications**, and **legal support**.

Contact Info:

📞 +230 211 4400

✉ hicom.mru@mea.gov.in

🌐 www.hcimauritius.gov.in

Additional Resources for Travelers

Beyond emergency services, a variety of online resources and apps can help you navigate Mauritius:

1. Mauritius Tourism Website

For **detailed information** about **events, attractions,** and **tourist services,** the official **Mauritius Tourism Authority website** is an essential resource.

Website: www.tourism-mauritius.mu

2. My Mauritius Mobile App

This free app offers real-time **tourist information, location-based services,** and **interactive maps** to guide you through the island.

Available on: iOS & Android

3. Emergency Alert Apps

There are apps like **Red Cross Mauritius** that send out **alerts** and provide **important safety tips** in the event of **natural disasters** or emergencies.

Conclusion

Knowing how to access key contacts and resources during your trip to Mauritius can help you stay informed, prepared, and safe. With these essential numbers and resources at your fingertips, you can enjoy everything Mauritius has to offer with **peace of mind**, knowing that **help is just a call away**.

CHAPTER SIXTEEN

RECOMMENDED TOUR OPERATORS AND GUIDES, ONLINE RESOURCES, AND APPS FOR TRAVELERS

As you plan your 2025 adventure in **Mauritius**, having the right resources at hand is key to making the most of your trip. Whether you're seeking expert guidance from a **local tour operator**, navigating the island with a **helpful app**, or exploring destinations via **online resources**, this chapter provides everything you need to ensure an unforgettable and smooth travel experience.

Recommended Tour Operators and Guides

Mauritius is a destination brimming with culture, adventure, and natural beauty, and working with a **local tour operator** can enhance your experience. From **beach tours** to **wildlife expeditions**, the island has a wide array of experienced tour operators ready to cater to your interests. Many of these operators offer **customized itineraries** and **expert guides** who are familiar with the island's hidden gems and historical landmarks.

Here are some highly recommended tour operators and guides for 2025:

Mauritian Wildlife Foundation

For eco-conscious travelers interested in Mauritius' **rich biodiversity**, the **Mauritian Wildlife Foundation** is an excellent option. This non-profit organization focuses on **conservation projects** and offers specialized **wildlife tours**. Take a guided trip to visit **endangered species**, **bird sanctuaries**, and **protected areas**. Their **local guides** provide in-depth knowledge of the island's ecosystems and conservation efforts.

Contact Info:

📞 +230 433 1446

✉ info@mauritian-wildlife.org

🌐 www.mauritian-wildlife.org

Mauritius Nature Walks

For a **personalized walking experience**, **Mauritius Nature Walks** offers private, guided hikes through the island's **lush rainforests** and **mountain ranges**. This operator is ideal for travelers who want to explore the island's more **remote landscapes**, from **Le Morne Brabant** to the **Black River Gorges**. Their guides provide extensive insights into **local flora and fauna**, as well as the island's history and culture.

Contact Info:

📞 +230 5782 2680

✉ info@mauritiusnaturewalks.com

🌐 www.mauritiusnaturewalks.com

Sunil Tours Mauritius

For those looking for **luxurious experiences** or **private tours, Sunil Tours Mauritius** offers top-notch, tailor-made packages. Specializing in **luxury transfers, private charters**, and **multi-day excursions**, this operator ensures that you experience Mauritius in style. Whether you're interested in a **sunset catamaran cruise** or a **private tour of the island's best beaches**, Sunil Tours guarantees a memorable journey.

Contact Info:

📞 +230 465 7600

✉ sunil@suniltours.com

🌐 www.suniltours.com

Pure Ocean Mauritius

For travelers who want to **dive deep** into the island's waters, **Pure Ocean Mauritius** offers **snorkeling** and **scuba diving excursions**.

Their guides are certified experts who lead tours in the **world-famous coral reefs**, making it a perfect choice for both beginner and advanced divers. They also provide information on sustainable diving practices to ensure that the natural environment is respected and preserved.

Contact Info:

📞 +230 5724 1535

✉ info@pureoceanmauritius.com

🌐 www.pureoceanmauritius.com

LUX Resorts and Hotels Tours

For travelers staying at *LUX Resorts** across Mauritius, the hotel offers guided **island tours**, **cultural experiences**, and **culinary excursions**. Their **private guides** take guests on bespoke experiences, exploring the best of Mauritius, from **tropical forests** to **traditional Creole villages**. LUX is perfect for those looking for a **luxurious yet immersive experience**.

Contact Info:

📞 +230 204 2222

✉ luxmauritius@luxresorts.com

🌐 www.luxresorts.com

Online Resources and Apps for Travelers

In today's digital world, having access to the right **online resources** and **travel apps** is essential for navigating a destination effectively. These tools help you access **real-time information, maps, local recommendations,** and **emergency contacts** right at your fingertips. Whether you're planning a **custom itinerary** or need **real-time advice** on weather and **local events**, here are some useful online resources and apps for Mauritius in 2025:

Mauritius Tourism Official Website

For a comprehensive overview of **Mauritius** including **accommodation options, activities, restaurants,** and **local events**, the official **Mauritius Tourism Authority** website is a must-visit. With up-to-date information on **weather forecasts, special promotions,** and **new attractions**, this site is perfect for those who want to **plan their trip in detail**.

Website: www.tourism-mauritius.mu

My Mauritius App

The **My Mauritius** app is a must-have for your trip in 2025. Available on **iOS** and **Android**, the app provides users with **interactive maps, restaurant guides, local activities**, and a **digital itinerary planner**. Whether you're exploring the **beaches, mountains**, or **cultural sites**, this app is an essential tool for navigating the island.

Available on: iOS & Android

Mauritius Travel Guide by TripAdvisor

If you rely on **crowd-sourced reviews** for recommendations, the **Mauritius Travel Guide by TripAdvisor** app is an excellent choice. It features **up-to-date reviews** on **hotels, attractions, restaurants**, and **excursions** from fellow travelers. The app also includes **interactive maps, filterable search options**, and tips for avoiding **tourist traps**.

Available on: iOS & Android

Google Maps

For **navigating Mauritius** with ease, **Google Maps** remains one of the most reliable tools.

From **driving directions** to **public transport routes**, **Google Maps** will help you get around the island hassle-free. The app is constantly updated with the latest **traffic conditions** and **road closures**, ensuring that your trip remains **smooth and stress-free**.

Available on: iOS & Android

Beach Locator by Mauritius

This specialized app focuses on the **beaches of Mauritius**, offering information on the best spots for **swimming, surfing, snorkeling,** and other water sports. The app also provides details on **facilities, accessibility,** and **crowd levels**, ensuring you find the perfect beach for your needs.

Available on: iOS & Android

Mauritian Emergency Assistance App

Designed for **safety-conscious travelers**, this app provides quick access to **local emergency numbers**, **hospital contacts**, and **nearest police stations**. It also offers **first-aid tips, emergency alerts,** and **weather updates**, ensuring you're well-prepared for any unforeseen situation.

Available on: iOS & Android

Conclusion

By tapping into the services of **trusted tour operators**, using the **best apps**, and visiting the right **online resources**, you will have everything you need to navigate **Mauritius** in 2025. These tools ensure that your trip is not only enjoyable but also **efficient** and **safe**. Whether you're looking for **local guides**, exploring the island independently, or seeking **emergency services**, you'll be well-equipped to make the most of your time in this **tropical paradise**.

Dear Traveler,

As you reach the final pages of *Mauritius Travel Guide 2025*, I just want to take a moment to say **thank you**—truly, from the bottom of my heart. It has been an absolute honor to be a part of your journey, guiding you through the wonders of this breathtaking island.

I hope this book has been more than just a guide—I hope it has inspired you, helped you uncover hidden gems, and made your adventure in Mauritius even more special. Whether you found yourself lost in the beauty of its turquoise waters, indulging in the island's incredible flavors, or connecting with its warm and welcoming people, I sincerely hope this trip has left you with memories to last a lifetime.

Travel has a unique way of opening our hearts and minds, and I am beyond grateful that you chose this book to accompany you on your journey. Your trust and support mean everything, and I hope this guide has lived up to your expectations.

If this book has helped you in any way, I would love to hear about your experiences! Your feedback, reviews, and stories mean the world to me and help fellow travellers just like you. Please consider leaving a review—it not only supports my work but also helps others make the most of their own Mauritius adventure.

Thank you again for allowing me to be part of your travels. Wherever your next adventure takes you, may it be just as incredible, exciting, and fulfilling. Until we meet again—happy travels, and may your journey always be filled with discovery and joy!

With heartfelt gratitude,

Jenny M. Dobson

NOTE:

Mauritius Travel Guide 2025

Printed in Great Britain
by Amazon